In Love With Humanity

Turning Every Adversity into an Opportunity

KS Chhabra

Life Story of KS Chhabra
as told to
Pradeep Bhinde

INDIA · SINGAPORE · MALAYSIA

ISBN 979-8-89133-611-7

First Edition: 27th November, 2022

Second Edition: 30th September, 2023

Cover Pages Design By: Tushar Nathani

tusharlnathani@gmail.com

KS Chhabra

kschhabra9@gmail.com

+91 9824010910

Price: Rs. 299/-

Dedicated To

My Parents – **The Late Shri Charan Singhji & Smt. Virender Kaur.**

My Guru – **Guruji Shri G. Narayana.**

My Wife – **Kawaljeet** – Companion in this beautiful journey.

Our Daughters – **Namrata and Amrit.**

Brahmakumari **Meena Didi**, Brahmakumar **Jitubhai Patel** – the Angels who came to enlighten the path.

Preeti Chandan – who played cupid between me and spirituality, showed me the illuminated path which led to my transformation.

All my **Anand Ashram friends** and dedicated volunteers who, all together, have contributed tremendously in making me what I am today!

Pradeep Bhinde and **Tushar Nathani** – this book will not have been possible without them.

IN LOVE WITH HUMANITY

Kawaljit Singh Chhabra was born in 1958 at Kanpur, Uttar Pradesh, India. He did his B.Pharm. and Post-Graduation in Management. KS Chhabra was a successful industrialist in the field of pharmaceutical formulations manufacturing. At the age of 53, he renounced his flourishing business and decided to dedicate rest of his life in service to humanity full time. His brain-child "Anand Ashram Charitable Trust" is a leading NGO today.

Shri Chhabra has been in various Managing Committees of some of the most prestigious institutions like Confederation of Indian Industries (CII), Federation of Gujarat Industries (FGI), Baroda Management Association (BMA), Indian Drugs Manufacturers' Association (IDMA), MS University Students' & Staff Union, Department of Pharmacy – MS University of Baroda, President – Rotary Club of Baroda Jawaharnagar, Founder Chairman-Alkapuri Jaycees Youth Club, President – MS University Pharmacy Alumni Association. He also represented India as part of Indo-Canadian Youth Exchange Programme.

His father, The Late Charan Singh Chhabra who served Reserve Bank of India, and mother Virender Kaur, have three sons: Kawaljit Singh, Col. Narendrajit Singh and Paramvir.

Identically named Kawaljeet is his wife. They have two daughters: Namrata who is a Biotechnologist, married to Debanjan Chakraborty, have a daughter Meher and son Aditya. All of them are Australian citizens.

Younger daughter Amrit is married to Yaksh Thakkar, a practising Advocate. They have a daughter, Mira. Amrit was a Management Consultant and now a social entrepreneur, Director – WellnessMantra, a company marketing Ayurveda wellness products.

Presently, KS Chhabra is serving the humanity as Managing Trustee of Vadodara's leading NGO Anand Ashram Charitable Trust which is engaged in number of social services. Anand Ashram has a volunteer base of talented people from all walks of life.

Contents

Foreword *9*

Preface *15*

1. The Turning Point 17
2. En Caul Baby! 25
3. The Litmus Test 35
4. The Untold Secrets 49
5. If Taj Mahal Stands for its Beauty, Chhabra Stands for His Duty! 63
6. Dream Enormously Big – Progress Knows No Bounds 71
7. Deh Shiva Bar Mohe Ihey, Shubh Karman Te Kabahu Na Taron! 85
8. The Art of Risking 95
9. Stable and Able 103
10. Rise and Recharge 115
11. In Love with Humanity 129
12. The Big Sewa Dream 147

Book Reviews *155*

Foreword

Dear Dear Kawaljit + Kawaljeet! AUM and PREM. Abhinandan and admiration for creating the wonderful divine book "In Love with Humanity" which is full of knowledge, information, ideas and solutions for starting, striving, struggling and succeeding in journey called *life*.

Dear Chhabraji, your starting, birth, was a miracle at Kanpur.

Your striving for success in education and examinations was mastery with mischievousness.

Your struggling, profession and business contributions were magnificent with meaningfulness.

Your succeeding in both industry and *sewa* is magnanimous grace of *Bhagwanji* who always remained with you openly and secretly and strengthened your Hands, Heels, Head and Heart.

Hands for working and making valuable contributions.

Heels for walking swiftly and smartly on known and unknown paths, whether your feet were normal, injured, bandaged or recovered. With the help of Dr. KT Dholakia, Dr.VM Shah and *Dr. Bhagwanji*, you proved your favourite phrase: "If Taj Mahal stands for beauty, Chhabra stands for duty!"

Head for always thinking, thinking and generating wonderful ideas and solutions like passing exams with help of brilliant partners, choosing and getting important jobs and roles, gaining a divine helpful life partner, in spirit of missed and declined opportunities for you. Head also worked for you in many solutions including bouncing back in business. In offering multiple partnership, you had transcended from being "owner" to "partner" with many, including your brother Paramvir, whose name is right for him because of his support and commitment for you.

Heart for your love for humanity at all stages of life expressed in most practical way of Serve and Deserve. You served people and rightly deserved the grace of elders and *Bhagwanji* Himself!

At each point and stage, you used your Hands, Heels, Head and Heart to transform adversity into advantage, chaos into clarity, problem into solution and crisis into championship!

The book is full of guidelines of wisdom, wit, winning way and wealth for all, which include:

1. "My trust in the fact that one can convert adversity into advantage is total." – Preface.

2. "I felt dizzy but I was conscious and upon realizing that we all were alive (after the serious accident) could not control my yelling and screaming voice shouting: "Thank you *Bhagwanji*" "Thank you *Bhagwanji*" "Thank you *Bhagwanji*"-Ch.1
3. "Sardars are generally not over-thinking types. Decisions are prompt! *"Jo bole so nihal!"* Ch.2
4. "Neither success, nor failure are ever final. It is courage that counts." Ch.3
5. "Goodwill, love, kindness, relations, bonding or whatever we call it – it is the mightiest force in the universe. If one cannot buy it and it has to be earned, then I have earned it!" Ch.3
6. "Ninety percent of leadership is the ability to communicate something people want." Ch.5
7. "Shoot for the moon. Even if you miss, you will land among stars." Ch.6
8. "O Lord Shiva! Give me this boon to never shirk from doing right." Ch.7
9. "True blessings always work. Golden words can change life." Ch.8
10. "During those unforgettable moments, I experienced the peace which I had known never before. A hurricane of negative forces had passed by me and I had survived the storm one more time."

"The great spiritual beginning was made. Beginning of greatest learning in spiritual world, *sthitpragyata* – Stable and Able!" Ch.9

11. "*Jo prapt hai, wo paryapt hai.*" Ch.10
12. "Now it was my responsibility to become a giver. I started that and He started helping me by sending contributors at Anand Ashram. I became instrumental in serving humanity. When you become giver from receiver, you become God's own representative." Ch.11

Dear Kawaljit + Kawaljeet! When you transform from receiver to offeror, you literally become an example of spirit of:

"Asatoma Sadgamaya, Tamasoma Jyotirgamaya, Mrityorma Amrtitamgamaya,

Ahantaya Atmagamaya!" Shubham Bhooyat!

The presentation, language and arrangement of chapters and spirit of communication in interpersonal humorous language is excellent, enjoyable and enrichingly informative.

My admiration and deep appreciation to both our Dear Kawaljit and our Dear Pradeep Bhinde with love and delight.

Pradeep has added great value to quality of narration with his lucid style of writing.

This unputdownable book is bound to be a super hit of great inspiration to people of all ages because it is almost life in all phases!

Namaste to All!

– G. NARAYANA

Preface

The Mighty Fall!

My trust in the fact that one can convert adversity into opportunity is total. The most recent incident in my life is the proof.

On 2nd February, 2022 afternoon, I stepped out in our compound on a slippery surface with my bulky body and I slipped. It was just like *Humpty-Dumpty had a great fall!* Landed up with two fractures on the same leg where I have a limp due to my earlier six surgeries. I thanked God that he saved my life as I escaped any head or hip injury.

Since last two years I had 'booked' Pradeep to sit with me to start narrating sessions to write this book, but due to busy schedules, the opportunity was not coming forth. Operation was performed thrice on my leg and after few days, I rang him:

"Bhindeji! I am seeing an opportunity in adversity!"

Pradeep knows me well; he immediately understood the underlying meaning of my sentence.

"Great! We can start from today itself!" He replied without even asking what I meant! Creative writing is his passion.

And now the book is in your hands. Opportunity grabbed! Interestingly, I used to completely forget my pain during our daily three hours' narration sessions at my home. If you don't feed the pain with your attention, pain becomes your friend.

The journey of life is like roller coaster ride.

This journey also has zigzag paths with many twists and turns, some known and some unknown. Challenging times come intermittently in everyone's life. When we live in happy times, they pass very fast. When we have to face unhappy times, they appear as if they are there to stay forever. In fact, nothing in life is permanent. Good or bad, both times pass because life is not static. Life is a flux. The sole intention of writing my life story is to inspire the youth and the children to prepare them for varied times of life.

My Beloved Youth and Children: One day you will tell your story of how you have overcome what you are going through now, and it will become someone else's survival guide!

– KS Chhabra

1.

The Turning Point

Some storms come just to clear a path.

Believe it or not!

Do you believe that ghosts or spirits exist? I never believed it. I still do not.

But wait! Spirits do exist!

The above may sound contradictory, but I am compelled to say so due to my own experience.

What was that *which* or perhaps *who* constantly was warning me against going for a picnic the next day?

Some background to the kind of life style our family led in my 50s will be needed here. Most of the leading hoteliers in city of Vadodara knew KS Chhabra family. Life was all about having full-on fun and frolic.

Though money was not in so much abundance, enjoyment was on top priority. Outings and picnics at new places were planned much before each holiday. Sundays invariably were picnic days.

How to enjoy life? Look at Chhabra couple! Friends used to say.

My mother-in-law was visiting us with my sister-in-law's 19-year-old daughter Ritu. Amrit, our daughter was just 9 at that time.

The incident which I am going to narrate here dates to year 1999.

This was the year when India had won Kargil war with Pakistan in July. The country was in euphoria with Shri Atal Bihari Vajpayee at the helm of affairs as PM in New Delhi.

We had planned a family picnic with these guests to Jojwa Check Dam site which is around 50 kms from Vadodara. Kumkum Bhardwaj, a dear friend Raman's wife had recommended and guided us about the spot.

On Saturday, the day prior, everyone was excited and ladies and children started making preparations for the picnic of Sunday, 21st November, 1999.

Truth is stranger than fiction indeed.

On previous night, no one in the family had slightest idea how from my bed room I landed on a large sofa in our drawing room!

No. I had not consumed alcohol. Nor did I have any history of sleep walking.

What followed was the strangest experience of my life. From this point, some unknown voice from within started giving me warning signals. It was a feeling as if some invisible force had possessed me who was communicating to me a clear message: *Drop the idea of going to Jojwa.*

To my utter disbelief, slowly the signals changed from persuasion to commands. I tried to whisk them away and go to sleep but their increased pace had taken over me.

The feeling of some invisible *presence* inside me was so tangible that I was inclined to believe that this must be some kind of friendly spirit who must have probably lifted me from my bed room to drawing room.

But strangely enough, it did not scare me. Maybe it was a kind of friendly spirit? I have no answer to this till date.

Somehow, I managed to again go to sleep around early morning.

The fateful Sunday dawned. On waking up I instantly noticed that previous night's inner voice had become clearer and now sterner too. Its force increased with the ongoing food and other preparations in the house. So much so that it started cursing in rage to stop us from going to picnic anyhow!

It was difficult for me to cancel the trip as it would disappoint the whole family, especially the children.

And the reason which I would give them would sound silly too.

Hey you! Enough. We are going. Please leave me alone! I muttered. I did not have the slightest idea about what I was overlooking.

It was a bright and sunny winter day. We had Premier 118NE car, a sturdy, robust and one of the safest cars of those times. But for this particular picnic, we chose my wife Kawaljeet's newly purchased red Maruti Zen for a smooth, thrilling drive.

With everything ready and the family excited for yet another joyful picnic ride, I took the driver's seat and put the key in ignition. To our utter surprise, the newly purchased car would not start! Surely an unusual thing to happen. One, two, three, four, five starters and the car refused to budge.

For a moment, my suppressed thoughts about some unknown lurking danger surfaced but putting a brave front, I managed them to push aside.

After few seconds' wait, the car started at the sixth effort. None of us had slightest idea that we were on our way to meet our combined fate very soon.

Mai zindagi ka sath nibhata chala gaya... is one of my favourite Hindi film songs which played on car's music system with volume full-on and the tempo was built once the car picked up the speed.

This way, perhaps I wanted to shadow the signals of friendly spirit which had now turned into soft whispers in a pleading manner:

Telling you for the last time, return from here. This last *call* was received by me while climbing an over bridge in the outskirts of Vadodara city from where we would be driving towards Dabhoi road to meet our destiny.

The urging, pleading, persuading inner voice had suddenly become silent as if it was subdued by the speeding car.

The car was running smoothly now on Vadodara-Dabhoi State Highway having covered almost half the distance to the picnic spot.

And it happened.

I suddenly saw two monstrous looking trucks from our opposite side in front racing to overtake each other.

Before I could realize what was happening, one truck fully loaded with sand which was running parallel with another one but could not overtake it, rushed like a mad bull towards our car.

It was exactly at this point where my conscious mind froze and by a robotized action common with all drivers, I turned the steering wheel towards side of the road and lost complete control. The car *flew* like a flying saucer in the air and banged against the thick trunk of a huge old tree in a near fatal crash.

Screams, cries of pain, the sudden loud boom of car made lots of people of nearby village and farms rush towards us with their farming tools like sticks, bamboo sieve, spade etc. to help.

They managed to break the widow glasses, cut open the jammed doors and immediately checked each one of us whether we were breathing. To me all of them appeared as form of God and in the tragic situation which we were in also, I had a glimpse of realization that He is omnipresent.

My mind was still not fully alert. Loud voices of people talking and uttering under their breath that it is impossible that anyone could survive after such accident made my heart sink.

I felt dizzy but I was conscious and upon realizing that we all were alive, could not help control my yelling and screaming voice shouting loudly *Thank you Bhagwanji, Thank you Bhagwanji, Thank you Bhagwanji* (Thank you God).

Exactly at this point when village people were discussing what could be done to get us medical help, an ambulance miraculously appeared on the road in a ditto Bollywood Movie style!

The ambulance was taking a pregnant lady from nearby town Dabhoi to Sir Sayajirao General Hospital at Vadodara city. Our saviors stopped the ambulance and all of us were lifted and put inside.

Amongst great pain, anxiety and fear I strangely felt a psychological relief too. The burden, the commanding voice from within, the feeling of being possessed although by a friendly spirit had gone.

How did I know?

Difficult to explain but it was something like the huge sense of relief you get when a heavy load is taken down from your chest. It never came back.

Was it some kind of intensified premonition which stopped after the accident?

Frankly, I have not been able to find an answer. There are numerous unexplained mysteries of life and this may be one.

The ambulance started immediately. Glancing from the window, it was painful to look at the remains of the car which was in a horrible shape and then also at the badly injured dear ones.

When the ambulance turned back towards Vadodara city, there was no indication at all that a turning point in my life was also on the horizon.

The storm had come to clear the path in my life.

2.

En Caul Baby!

An en caul birth is when the baby comes out still inside an intact amniotic sac (caul). This might make it look like your newborn is completely gift wrapped in a soft, jello-like bubble.

"A baby who is born lucky" according to Biblical Mythology

"This child is going to be very lucky. He will do meaningful tasks for the humanity."

Sister Lawrence exclaimed beaming with surprise and excitement.

I was in her hands! New born with my gift wrapper intact!

30th September, 1958. Early morning 3.45 am. Kanpur. On the banks of India's most sacred river Ganga!

The scene was at the time of my birth in Mission Hospital. Kanpur is a large city in Uttar Pradesh State of India. It was one of the most important commercial and military stations of British India. Even today Kanpur stands as the major financial and industrial centre of North India and the ninth largest urban economy in India.

This type of birth is in fact, an extremely rare phenomena and Sister Lawrence linked it with Biblical mythology which describes such child as the one cut out to serve the humanity.

Shri Charan Singh Chhabra, my father served there with Reserve Bank of India.

My father repeated this story to me and all our friends and relatives throughout his life till he passed away at the age of 93 in 2022, that when I was born, I came out of the womb with amniotic sac wrapped around me intact. Such births are rare and such children are most lucky children. Every time I achieved something in life too, may it be on academic, business or sewa front, he used to repeat the story with the same excitement!

He always took pride over this unusual happening and noticing my ever readiness for always helping others, he expressed it to me on many occasions and blessed me to scale great heights in that direction.

I was grown as pampered child. Love was overflowing all around in the family for me.

My *nani* (mom's mom) always pampered me and would go on stuffing my tummy with my favourite mashed boiled potatoes smeared with butter. I have observed this in Punjabi families that children are pampered too much by their elders, especially grandparents. This does more harm than good to the little ones. The fat cells which are formed due to such calorie rich food stay there forever. Starving yourself is the only remedy then.

I am paying the price of such pampering even today as obesity has stayed my loyal companion throughout my life!

From the early age, I was a jolly go-getter. I could make friends easily and was quite popular among them.

Kanpur saw me as a small kid only. Memory of a school at Kanpur is associated with a funny incident during our visit there in summers when my maternal aunt Tripta had taken me to her school. Tripta *masi* was a school teacher and once she had taken me to her class.

When we reached the school and she entered the class with me and made me seat on one of the last benches, I distinctly remember having provided hilarious moments to the entire class.

In between when she was teaching, I suddenly stood up from the bench and asked her in front of the whole class:

"*Tripta masi, Tu meri nicker toh daingi?*" (Would you wash my nicker?).

Obviously, I had done potty in my nicker in the class!

She took me to toilet leaving rest of the students in the class chuckling and giggling.

One more incident was with my Nani, during such summer visit. In Kanpur, easiest means of transport during those days was cycle rickshaw. We were going somewhere in it. Such rickshaws are driven by men pedaling in front with passengers seated on back.

On the way, I saw some piglets playing on the road side.

"Who are those *nani*?" I was curious.

"Kids of *suvvar* (pig)" *Nani* replied.

"Wow! How cute are they!" I was fascinated and clapped with my little hands. I do it even today when I am fascinated to something or someone, of course now with my big hands!

She quipped: "*Ek suvvar da bacha* (one such piglet) is here with me too!"

I was still a kid when my father was transferred to Ahmedabad in Gujarat State where I was admitted to study in a Municipal School. The only "significant" memory I have of this school is that we had to carry our own glass to school for drinking milk which was served to children in Municipal Corporation schools then. Once my glass had fallen on a dirty ground where all the kids used to urinate unitedly in group!

Lessons of 'unity is strength' started at an early age!

At this small age also, I was saved from a near fatal injury while playing near a construction site. A huge stone debris fell upon me and almost buried me underneath.

Although I was saved, the nervous system of my kidneys was affected and it took long time to strengthen the system again. During this period, I suffered from bed-wetting which doctors assured that it will be cured once I grow little older.

God's protective umbrella was showing its presence.

Small incidents of innocent theft and smoking also made me see many colours of life.

There used to sit vendors outside all schools to sell flavourful items like Indian gooseberry and peppermints etc. Although they were not at all costly, but as we were given no pocket money, it was just empty treat to our eyes daily.

Once I stole a 25 paise coin from the house and bought my favourite eatables. But after returning home, I confessed to my mom what I did.

"Theft" not in its real sense but high-tech(!) examination cheating was to become my forte in college life later!

The crime of theft was pardoned but smoking a cigarette was not. Pravesh, son of my father's friend

Shri HP Pandey, once offered me to smoke a cigarette when both our moms had gone to vegetable market. Although we had opened all windows of the room and enjoyed the first-time experience of smoking, both moms immediately knew what we did in their absence. We both were punished to sleep outside the house for the night.

Leadership qualities have been God-gifted to me right from KG! In school, I remained an average student as all my energies and time were diverted to other creative activities rather than studies. Anything other than studies, my name was always on tip of the tongues of my teachers.

Need a monitor? Kawal.

Need a class representative? Kawal.

Extracurricular activities like drama, sports, picnics, event management? Kawal.

I had developed soul-mate kind of relationship with one of our teachers, Mrs.Kadri. The relationship had started with her hard slap!

I was very fond of swimming but its timings and the school timings clashed. Also, school was located at Delhi Chakla at Ahmedabad and Municipal swimming pool was at Lal Darwaza. So, I started bunking her Chemistry classes.

Noticing my continuous absence, Mrs. Kadri started investigating the reasons and found out from others that I had bunked all her classes to learn swimming. I was summoned by her in the class and in front of all the students, she slapped and scolded me. Her slap changed me but my bonding with her became extremely strong after that. I have no clue where she is now, but my soul-to-soul relation with Mrs. Kadri will remain forever.

My more memories of schooling although have faded with passing of time, but the lessons learned in the school of life are unforgettable.

One such funny incident happened due to my mischief in train.

Kanpur being the city of my maternal relatives, my *mama* (maternal uncle) Gurdeep Singh once came to Ahmedabad to take us to Kanpur. This was our custom that *mama* will come to take us along with our mom and other siblings and then come for dropping us back too.

We boarded a train which was going from Ahmedabad to Delhi. It was a 3-tier compartment of a class known as 3rd Class at that time and my berth was at the top.

This was the first time that I noticed a chain with handle hanging near me.

"What is this *mamaji*?" I wanted to know.

"*Putter* (my son), it is called chain. If we pull it, the train will stop"

Gurdeep *mama* repented immediately after parting his *gyan* to me because he was well-versed with my devilish adventures.

I didn't say anything to him at that time but started pondering over and over how such a huge train can be stopped by just pulling such a small chain!

There must be some magic. Let me try! Will somebody scold me? Police might arrest me?

Sardars are generally not over-thinking types. Decisions are prompt! *Jo bole so nihaal!*

At midnight, when passengers were asleep, fed up with confused thoughts but tremendously attracted by the idea of stopping a train, I pulled the chain!

My God! The train started slowing down and, in a while, it really stopped!

I had stopped a fast-running train!

Gurdeep *mama* was confident it was me and quickly tried a trick to save me.

The moment Guard came to our compartment to check who did it, he started shouting:

"*Pakdo..Pakdo* a guy has escaped after pulling the chain from our compartment"

In the hustle bustle that followed, everyone was convinced by his theory including the Guard that some mischief monger had escaped and at the top berth, I was wondering whether something will now happen to me?

I heaved a sigh of relief when the Guard left and Gurdeep mama only showed his wide eyes and his threatening slap to me as he had no choice but to keep mum in front of others.

The night passed with thrilled feeling of doing a great mammoth task of stopping a train!

Coach of the train became my life-coach!

3.

The Litmus Test

Neither success, nor failure are ever final. It's courage that counts.

Heading for the bigger accident – in Operation Theatre itself!

My first "direct-talk" with God!

Let us catch the thread of what happened after our near fatal accident.

When Paramvir, my younger brother contacted someone who had knowledge about the accident site, he provided a scary and chilling information. He informed that every year people die in fatal accidents near that particular spot named *Fartikui* on Dabhoi road near Vadodara.

How Chhabra family survived is a mystery. Death was inevitable at that spot as it is possessed by some evil spirit which requires sacrifices every year.

"Now please go there once again on their behalf and leave a live cock and bottle of desi alcohol under the tree. Do not look back" He suggested.

Paramvir arranged to perform the ritual promptly.

The worst major injuries were suffered by Ritu, my sister-in-law's daughter and me. Her head was broken and the skull was split open with brain protruding out of it.

My mother-in-law had fractured her both legs.

Kawaljeet, my wife's one side of the body had turned blue.

My right leg was badly stranded between steering wheel and dash-board. The least sufferer was our daughter Amrit who only had a smashed bleeding nose and cut lips.

Amrit was just 9 at that time and she took command of the situation bravely. We were happily surprised seeing her calm and composed conduct in such gory situation.

Everyone, just everyone, survived miraculously!

God's protective umbrella was safeguarding us all.

Ritu had to undergo complicated surgery but it was successful and she survived.

My mother-in-law, Kaushalyadevi was referred to private hospital for treatment. Due to fractures in both legs, she had to use a walker for lifetime after operation.

As Kawaljeet had no significant injury but half of her body had turned blue due to impact of the collision, she was given first aid type of treatment and was not hospitalized. She was alright after few days.

My right leg bone (Femur) was broken into 13 pieces. At SSG Hospital, doctors opined that this is a case of amputation of leg.

I was admitted to one of Vadodara's well-known hospitals, Bhailal Amin General Hospital where a young dashing doctor Dr. Harsha Hegde, Orthopedic Surgeon attended me.

After thorough examination, he opined that he can perform surgery but there are chances that the leg may have to be amputated; for this, my permission was needed.

"What will happen doctor if the operation is done without leg amputation?" I demanded.

"Death!" He replied with clinical detachment.

Direct *one-to-one* with Him!

Death? The reply of Dr. Harsha flung me to God's feet that night. I call this moment of my life as my first one-to-one 'encounter' with Him. He appeared instantly on remembering Him. I pleaded for His guidance.

Hey, Bhagwanji! Should I say yes for amputating my leg or not?

He gave a beautiful reassuring smile in reply.

I had got my answer.

Hospital management completed all the paper work and they took from me in writing that it was my own decision to carry out the surgery without amputation of my leg.

Destiny had some more packages ready in store for me.

I was transferred to OT and was put in lithotomy surgical position with my legs in slings tied on a stand. General anesthesia was introduced but I faintly started listening to piercing sound of drilling machine for a moment.

Meanwhile, due to some mysterious reasons not declared outside OT by the doctors, the requirement of blood became 30 units instead of 3 which Hospital had asked to keep ready initially. Near and dear ones had started contacting friends and relatives and by post-midnight, about 350 well-wishers thronged the hospital campus. They did not budge till the operation was over.

Strangely, the operation which started at 8.00 pm lasted till 4.00 am next day!

Goodwill, love, kindness, relations, bonding or whatever we call it. It is the mightiest force in the universe. If one cannot buy it and it must be earned, then I *had* earned it!

I have no words for all those people who remained with me in my difficult times. My love in abundance, my prayers for their well-being and my feelings of gratitude will always be there for them.

Well, the surgery without amputating my leg was over at last.

It was not successful but I was still alive! God's protective umbrella had once again safeguarded me.

The entire episode in OT gifted my body one more guest: Staphylococcus (Staph).

Staph is a group of bacteria that can cause several infectious diseases in various tissues of the body. Doctors say generally it is a 'hospital acquired infection' meaning that if something goes wrong during surgery, patient can get it.

I did get it!

During all the mess that happened during my operation, may be unsterilised surgical instruments were used or owing to any other unknown reason, I had become a victim of this one of the most stubborn infections.

The effect of Staph was continuous body fever which lasted for long period. No antibiotic would help. Doctors started looking for an international brand of it and they found out that it is available at Bangalore. This extremely costly antibiotic was ordered and it came to Vadodara by flight.

International antibiotic also failed.

A medical conference was arranged at the hospital to find out a solution. My bed was in the centre and top-notch doctors General Surgeon, Urologist, Orthopaedic, Physician, Blood Infection Specialist were also there discussing my mysterious fever.

Ultimately, doctors declared my condition as Pyrexia of Unknown Origin (PUO).

By this time, I had bounced back to my original witty self.

When the discussion ended, I politely asked whether I myself could offer a solution.

"Go ahead" Dr. Hegde said, looking at me, surprised!

"Look doctors! I have had no peg for more than two years. Give me a peg of Whisky along with your antibiotics. This will do the trick with all starved bacteria too!"

There were splits of laughter amongst doctors.

"Sure, why not?" Dr. Hegde quipped immediately.

"But that will be strictly under medical supervision!" He added.

Now it was my turn to laugh heartily. My fever went away in due course of time.

Bhailal Amin General Hospital finally washed their hands of the treatment.

We started searching the best Orthopaedic Doctors in Vadodara city and some of the top doctors examined me. Everyone was of the same opinion that this is a difficult case.

I started looking for the best in the country.

Incidentally, I have always believed in best of everything.

Put your best efforts in whatever you do. Success will inevitably follow.

Go for the best. If you have the freedom and resources to choose, always go for the best.

This search landed me to Mumbai to Dr. KT Dholakia who was visiting specialist at famous Breach Candy Hospital and Bombay Hospital too.

"Look Mr. Chhabra. I will make only one attempt as yours is really a bad case. You will have to be admitted and stay in Breach Candy for about two months. That will be the minimum period of your stay at Breach Candy."

No way! I shook my head.

"Doctor! This much long at Breach Candy will be very difficult and quite expensive for me." I pleaded "Kindly suggest a doctor of your stature in Gujarat"

Dr. Dholakia suggested a name at Jamnagar and that was Dr.VM Shah.

People at Jamnagar used to say about Dr.VM Shah's skill that if you take handful of broken bones to him in your palms, he will join them!

Well, my case was not *that* bad!

Dr.VM Shah examined me and was ready for surgery. He also said that he would make only one attempt. Period of hospitalisation would be maximum 10 days and expenditure around Rs.1.25 lakhs.

Thus, yet one more, sixth surgery, was done to repair my femur bone. Dr. Shah skilfully operated upon it and declared that it was successful.

What was the mystery that surrounded my operation inside the Operation Theatre of Bhailal Amin General Hospital? Why it took so long and why the requirement of blood became 30 units from 3?

The mystery was revealed after about four years of operation by my present Orthopaedic Surgeon who remembered my name when I first consulted him for post operation care treatment.

"Are you same Chhabra who was operated at Bhailal Amin General Hospital about four years back and where, during your operation, Hydraulic System had failed?" he asked.

O My God! What is he talking about? I did not have the slightest idea about any such mishap inside OT.

Hiding my ignorance, I nodded and asked: "Ji Sir. But how do you know about it?"

"Dr. Nagpal had discussed your case with me." The doctor replied.

Then he explained the functioning of Hydraulic System and what had happened.

Operation Theatre tables are designed to provide accurate positioning of patient's body during operation especially during surgical process that require precision. This system had failed during my operation! I must have remained hanging on the stand with my legs tied above.

This was indeed a shocking revelation.

I must be looking like a dead goat hanging at butchers! I was thinking. *Bhagwanji, do you sometimes enjoy such jokes too?!*

So, this was the reason why my operation took so long and the requirement of blood went on increasing.

My wife Kawaljeet still repeats her statement to friends: "More serious accident had taken place *inside* the Operation Theatre rather than on the road!"

During the three long years I stayed either in hospital or at home with my leg injury not capable of joining my business, two most fascinating things emerged in my life.

First, I learnt quickly that I had to make friends with my pain. One can always tackle the so-called disasters or challenges in life in two ways:

One way is that we curse our destiny and go on grumbling and complaining about what happened. When in pain, many people groan and moan and gurgle.

A better way, the positive way, is to accept whatever happens to us which is beyond our control and make friends with our situation.

Once this realisation dawned on me, I started accepting the situation quickly. Pain and me soon became good friends.

Acceptance is magical! Acceptance is love!

Once I made friendship with pain, its severity diminished.

The whole game is of altering your psyche due to which body starts releasing 'happy hormones' which helps in reducing the pain.

I have total faith in this 'acceptance' technique. It can help everyone endure not only pain, but tough situations in life also. Tough times do not last, tough people do.

I of course gained strength to accept the situations from my Almighty Friend! People worship him in temples and mosques and churches, whereas I claim to have direct one-to-one friendship, hugging-friends-like friendship with God!

Second positive outcome was fascinating indeed!

My wife, Kawaljeet, bravely came forward and took charge of our business!

I was astonished by her capabilities that emerged during the three years' time when she managed reins of home and business simultaneously! Challenges on home and business fronts were faced by her all alone! Both daughters Namrata and Amrit supported to their very best.

In our scriptures, it is mentioned that, *Nari Tu Narayani.* O Woman! You ARE Goddess! I saw and adored Kawal in this form of *Narayani.*

It will not be out of place here to make a mention of our happy married life.

In a world where the institution of marriage has been condemned, quarrels, marital crimes and divorce are rampant and where, in general it is believed that majority of married couples suffer due to wrong choices or non-adjustments, here also I proved to be one of the luckiest husbands.

We were always winner of the Best Couple awards at all such competitions.

Friends have been asking me the secrets of this success. I will reveal them here.

Kawal basically has a friendly nature. In our togetherness of almost 40 years, I have rarely seen any negativity in her.

But, as they say, man is a bundle of positivity and negativity both. That's quite human.

What is important is to consider the positivity and ignore the negativity. She happened to think in similar way and applied it to me as well!

Frank communication is another important aspect between the couples. We both have been able to achieve it and that is one golden key to happiness in marriage.

Taking care of each other's choices plays a great role. She is quite fond of outings, good food, good clothing. I suppose I have been always taking care of these things. Can you believe, I once bought 10 different coloured saaris for her on her birthday and the happiness I saw on her face was unforgettable!

We have moved across to see the world around to UK, Germany, Austria, France, Italy, Netherlands, Vatican City, Australia, New Zealand, most countries of UAE, Indonesia, Malaysia, Singapore, Thailand, Bhutan, Maldives.

Respect each other's relatives and maintain cordial relations with them equally. We both have followed this principle which has rewarded us by keeping our family bonds very strong.

Well, this does not mean that for the entire life we did not have frictions.

When I suffered from accident and was not mobile for almost 3 years and she started attending the factory to take care of business, she was not happy with the state of affairs there. Kawal is a perfectionist and I, being I, was running business in my own "its fine" "should be ok" style.

Kawal was furious after looking at what she thought were the "loopholes" in the business managed by me so far. This was the period when she used to remain upset with me as she found my ways of working not matching with her thought process at all.

Of course, the paradise was regained in due course as she bounced back to her original blissful self once everything was normal.

Marriages, as the saying goes, are made in heaven.

I say: Marriage, if these simple secrets are understood and applied, *is* heaven!

In due course after vigorous physiotherapy, I re-started walking on my own. No wheel chair, no walker, no walking stick. My right limb became shorter than the left by three inches, leaving a limp on right leg when I walk as my companion.

The student who evaded laboratory tests during studies was giving litmus test of life with courage!

4.

The Untold Secrets

My bold confessions. I made these mistakes. Make sure you do not.

"अपने मन का हो तो अच्छा, अगर न हो तो और भी अच्छा क्योंकि फिर वो ईश्वर के मन का होगा."

-स्व. हरिवंशराय बच्चन

Whenever Amitabh Bachchan fondly remembers these words of his great writer-poet father with this quote in his various interviews, it takes me down the memory lane of my own life.

Today I can make a bold statement that I have very few regrets in life, but the confessions that are going to follow here pricked my conscience for long.

The 'theft' about which I mentioned previously refers to cheating in exams.

Because of one clarity in my mind, I have remained an average student throughout my academic career.

The reason was obvious.

I had a clarity since early schooling that if someone wants to achieve big in life, the secret does not lie only in school books.

Learning life-lessons is equally or perhaps even more important than being a scholar or a gold medallist.

This was the reason all my energies were diverted to all the "full-of-life" activities and as a result, formal studies were compromised.

Even though, this did not mean that I neglected studies completely. No. Only that I never bothered to overcome my weak areas in studies; while I excelled in some subjects, Maths was a nightmare for me.

In studies, a student must pass in all subjects overcoming his weak areas. If he cannot do so, he is considered a failure. I have never subscribed to this thought in life. I believe this term 'failure' is a misnomer and discourages young minds.

It is your right attitude towards life, robust, outstanding personality that you develop, the level of self-confidence you gain; all these put together, lead you to success. I firmly believed and followed this.

And this was exactly the reason I never made efforts to improve in my weak subjects.

Here also, His ever-pervasive presence helped me. I had good teachers who were very considerate and sought to look out for me in class, not because of my scholarly traits but due to my humanitarian qualities. Except studies, I was everywhere: may it be debates, may it be dramas, may it be going and helping people in slum areas, may it be students' union elections.

Elections and their campaigns have always been my forte and I hardly have lost the elections. In fact, I lost only one election and I took it as a signal from above that he had reserved me for the opportunity that followed.

Now it had become the responsibility of my teachers not to let me fail! But it was pure love and affection that they always helped me. No underhand dealings or no money was ever involved. Solved question papers would reach my home and I used to cram the answers. This 'great' quality of cramming helped me in almost all my exams!

Now I had to give Board Exam of Old SSC.

This time my *Bhagwanji* inspired me from within to do hard work and I diligently concentrated and worked hard on all subjects like never before.

I passed SSC Board Exam with distinction! I also ranked 4th in my school! Everyone was surprised that an average student got more than distinction marks and a rank! I knew that hard work always pays, but still the area of formal education was never a priority for me.

At that time in whole Gujarat, it was every student's ambition to get admission in Maharaja Sayajirao University of Baroda (MSU). So was mine.

God always supports good and well-meaning ambitions. I wanted admission in Science Stream but there was an open test again for those who wanted admission there.

One more exam? But soon a decision came from the University that those who had got more than 70% marks in SSC will get direct admission in Science Stream.

That's how I got admitted in Preparatory Science at MS University of Baroda.

By the time I passed my SSC exams and entered college life, I invested my efforts not in studies, but in developing a charismatic humanitarian kind personality. Perhaps this was a bye-product generated from the mix of my ever-helping nature, friendly approach, positive thinking and yes, to a certain extent my personality which was, in the words of my friends of course, charismatic!

I was known as a handsome *sardar* (Sikh). I used to keep beard and wear turban. Females of course were quite fond of me too!

Interestingly, when I contested VP's election from the University, 94% vote share that I received was from girl students of Faculty of Home Science at MS University!

All my efforts were directed to develop these 'life-grooming' traits rather than studies.

One year of Preparatory Science passed in developing strong bonds with lecturers, other students, University authorities and students' welfare activities.

Finals of Preparatory Science arrived. For the first time in my academic career, I failed in Maths.

Why?

An absolutely unbelievable event had happened. I slept in the exam hall!

Actually my 'crafts' didn't work till previous day of exam so I consumed Dexamphetamine tablet the night before the Maths paper. This tablet stimulates the nervous system and keeps you awake. I tried to study and cram Maths course for the whole night and the moment I started writing my answer paper the next day, I slept in the exam hall.

God, perhaps, also slept this time and did not come to my rescue.

A rule of MS University saved my whole year. When a student passed in all subjects except one, he was granted "Allowed to Keep Term (ATKT)". He would have to clear it within six months though.

I entered First Year of B.Sc. and on clearing my ATKT, I was also eligible to opt for either Medical/ Engineering/Architecture/Pharmacy course. For getting admission to any of these courses, there was an All India Common Test. We could tick mark all or any number of courses of our choice. Except Medical, I tick marked all the rest. In fact, medical course was and even now it is, the topmost course in demand.

Yet another Test! This time All India Open Test!

Now?

The test was conducted at Faculty of Technology & Engineering where our examination hall had steps raised from front to back. So, writing tables had to be placed in theatre type arrangement.

Mahendra Nathdwarawala, (now Dr. Mahendra Nathdwarawala, well-known Cardiac Surgeon) a brilliant student and my most dear friend was seated on front seat, just before my seat.

"Mahendra dear! When you write a page, place it in my full view. When I say OK, turn it over and place aside."

Mahendra, who was going to be one of the finest Cardiologists of Vadodara in future, looked through his glasses to me with his intelligent eyes and nodded.

Result of All India Open Test?

Mahendra got 5th rank in merit!

KS Chhabra got 6th rank in merit!

I had absolutely no idea what were the questions asked in the question paper!

He went to Medical but as I had not opted for it, I got a choice to go for Engineering, the topmost course in demand after Medical.

Without giving much thought, I paid the fees and got admission in Engineering. Within a month I realized that I had committed a blunder. Maths was going to be integral part of engineering studies and how will I survive?

No. I must act fast. By this time, I had developed very strong bondage with Faculty Dean, Prof. SM Sen.

"Not possible, Chhabra. You can't change your stream now" Prof. Sen stubbornly refused my plea.

"Please Sir! You must help me. I have realized my blunder and my aptitude is different. For example, the smart, suited-booted, tie-sporting Medical Representatives have always carried an air of fascination for me. I can also see seeds of social service in myself and my going in pharmaceuticals may be useful to the society in future. Who knows, I may start my own medicines manufacturing facility to help the suffering humanity. Moreover, Biology, one of the important subjects of Pharma, is my strength too"

"So, you want to go to Pharma?" I could see Prof. Sen melting.

"Yes Sir. Please approve my change of stream". The Dean obliged.

And in 1978, the journey of my professional career began when I got admission in B.Pharm.

During college days also, my adventures during exams continued. They had to because in B. Pharm too, there were tough subjects which bothered me again.

Due to my reputation of humanitarian approach to the needy and ever ready to help attitude, God in the form of kind professors and loving colleagues was ever ready to help here too! Various methods were applied to help me ranging from calling me home to write the answer papers to changing my seats in exam hall with a clever student.

With challenges though, I sailed through the exams in university also.

I remember some interesting incidents.

University final exams were always strictly held. But there was an escape route for subjects like Maths in IInd Year where passing marks (36 marks) could save a student. There were 3 internal tests of 20 marks each. Best 2 of the 3 were to be considered. If you could score total 36 marks from 3 tests, they were added in final result. 36 was the magic figure for passing an exam. 4 marks were given as grace if you get 36. This meant that if you get even zero in finals, you will pass! I had got the key.

My game began with the 1st Internal Test of Maths.

Scene 1: My friend Dipti Jailwala was seated near me in the exam hall. She was too good in studies. Dipti allowed me to copy the answers. We both got same marks 18 out of 20.

Prof. Patel who taught us Maths rightly guessed what had happened. But as Chhabra was dear to all and quite famous, no action was taken.

Scene 2: With 18 marks in Maths now in my credit, I did not appear for the 2nd Internal Test at all.

Scene 3: Manipulating Third Internal Test of Maths proved to be very tough. Strict arrangements were made during the test just as they show in the movies where full-proof security of diamonds displayed in glass show-cases is provided.

The atmosphere was loaded with alertness during previous papers.

I started enquiring where are the papers printed? A particular professor (I cannot divulge the name because of obvious reasons) oversaw printing. I urged him to help but he said it is impossible. *Sorry Chhabra.*

But God was smiling again. Professor had a change of heart. In those times, papers were printed on cyclostyling machine. When he saw the final copies, he threw one copy in dustbin saying it was not printed properly. No one doubted. While closing the printing room, he trickily picked up the tossed away copy and reached my Hostel Room at 9.30 pm in the night!

In exchange, there was no expectation from his side. The currency of love and kindness was working.

But what about the answers of this paper? *Let's find a Maths wizard!*

And I found Kartik Dave. My closest of friends since school days.

Kartik solved the paper for me at night and I crammed it completely. As I said, cramming was my strength! I submitted my answers before everyone. Shocked. and surprised students and invigilator of course must have guessed something fishy!

I got 19 marks out of 20 which was highest in the class, and I was through in Maths as my internal test total was 37. Prof. Patel always wondered what kind of jugglery I had done. I always jocularly teased Kartik how could I lose that 1 mark? However, there was no need to bother about final exam of Maths now!

God once again was standing there with his protective umbrella! Smiling!

During my 3rd year of B. Pharm, story of my heroic achievements by manipulations in exams continued.

Element of drama was also introduced during final practical exam of Pharmacology. While I excelled in subjects like Hospital Pharmacy and others, Pharmacology gave me jitters.

The final practical exam was held in Laboratory under supervision of external invigilators. Here, my favourite professor, let us call him Prof. Angel, became my saviour. He had been helping me all these years and now was the finale.

By previous evening my fertile brain lit up with an idea and I slept relaxed. In the morning before the practical exam, I tied lots of bandages on my right hand and made it appear as if it was fractured.

I entered examination hall with my hand in sling and on seeing Prof. Angel, I started groaning as if I was suffering from unbearable pain.

"*Kya hua Chhabra*?" Prof. Angel came to me and enquired.

"Sir, I slipped on a wet floor and fractured my hand yesterday" I gave him my readymade answer without blink of an eye.

Professor was smart enough to guess that it was nothing but acting. All the same, he convinced the external invigilators to let me just sit on a side during the practical exam without doing anything!

Once they had left, he again came to me : "Hey, actor Chhabra! Now throw away all these bandages. I know you well. Chill, I have already told them that you are a good student and recommended that because of accident, you should be passed on sympathetic grounds"

This time I saw God burst out laughing instead of just smiling!

By the time final year of B. Pharm started, I had grown much mature. The realization that there is no substitute for hard work of course was always there. Soon, this attitude started paying rich dividends and I passed my last year exams without any of my tricks.

And now, my most important message here, especially for the youth.

Why have I confessed my exam manipulations here? They were in no way any great achievements or some kind of glorious deeds.

The reason is compassion.

I want to give a very important message to children and the youth, to student fraternity by confessions from my own life story.

Never ever go for manipulations. Always trust God's designs.

The paths which are charted for you by Him are the real path which are created by Him for your well-being.

Who knows that if I had not manipulated in exams, I may have got a better life awaiting me?

Deep down I have a strong confidence that if I would have improved upon my weak subjects by hard work rather than manipulations, I could have become one of the top-notch doctors. Admission in Medical was possible and I had to let it slip out of my hands just because I did not want to overcome my weaknesses.

When the dams are built at wrong places on the river, the result could be disastrous.

Accept with gratitude whatever comes to you from destiny.

Another situation needs a mention here.

I had a cousin sister, Mohinder Kaur at Ludhiana who was suffering from cancer. She had an ardent desire to meet me before she left her body. Owing to circumstances, I could not visit her till I received sudden news of her death.

For long. I was carrying a regret in my conscience. But then, the realisation did solace me that it could be God's wish not to make us meet. May be because of my own karma or her own deeds, our meeting was not to be taken place. This realisation did make me comfortable later on.

Remember, if your wish is fulfilled, good. If not, better. Because then it becomes God's wish!

5.

If Taj Mahal Stands for its Beauty, Chhabra Stands for His Duty!

> *"Ninety percent of leadership is the ability to communicate something people want."*

Communication skill has been my strongest USP since early age.

During my schooling, this trait was discovered by teachers in me. On all occasions like monitoring, leading sports teams, extra-curricular activities and the like, they utilised this quality of mine.

Experience at school became net practice for university.

At University, the canvas widened. Political parties have from the very beginning been involved in Maharaja Sayajirao University of Baroda elections. Good number of prominent political leaders have also emerged by net practice at university level elections.

Being elected as MS University's Faculty of Science Management Committee Representative in the very first year Preparatory Science was the beginning. By the end of year, I was well-known in university circles with a clean image and excellent reputation of a leader who always stood for humanitarian causes.

In First Year of B.Sc. in addition to being CR, I became Secretary, Cultural Activities & Publications and Secretary, Executive Committee Member of Boys' Hostel.

To every student who studied stayed in a hostel for studies, days spent during hostel life are unforgettable and full of fond memories.

Hostel life reminds me of a funny incident.

MM Hall of MS University where I stayed, is located near railway tracks and seeing the passing trains was a routine sight for us.

Once during exam days, I found I had no fresh pair of clothes and so I soaked my shirt and pants at night in soap water and got up at early morning around 4.00 am to air dry them.

I was hanging them on a string in the balcony when a scene on the railway track made me freeze with horror. What I saw was a train was passing on the tracks and it was burning. Yes, flames were coming out of the compartment and it was still running!

My God! This must have happened after it left the railway platform. I must inform the authorities.

Without much thinking I picked up my wretched bicycle, started pedalling fast and rushed towards railway station to inform the Station Master. I had to pass the same tracks where I saw the train burning.

Suddenly, I saw the train stopping. I saw full star cast of the famous Bollywood movie "The Burning Train" coming out of it near the tracks! Dharmendra, Hema Malini, Vinod Khanna, and Jitendra!

Mention of my tatty bicycle reminds me how the thought of returning a paltry sum of Rs.50 to my bicycle repairer kept nagging my conscience. The bicycle wala knew my parents were at Jaipur and I kept on visiting there. Once he requested me to bring bearings from Jaipur's National Bearing Company and gave me advance for it. When I got him the bearings, Rs.50 were to be returned by me to him and I did not have the change. So, the matter was forgotten.

After about 5 years' gap, when I was in Vadodara, I made it a point to locate him and return his money. He although never remembered it, but I was happy to clear my conscience. This purity I have always tried to maintain in my life and never ever I have asked, borrowed, or taken anyone's money unduly. I may, of course must have given it in excess many a times!

This honesty has always kept me at peace with myself.

Meanwhile, climbing the leadership ladder at university continued. I became Faculty Representative (FR) when

I took change in Pharmacy at Faculty of Engineering & Technology.

The campus of this faculty is beautiful with lush gardens inside it. The huge dome of the central building is famous for its architecture. Faculty was formed along with establishment of MS University in 1949. It is an outgrowth of what was popularly known as the Kala Bhavan Technical Institute (KBTI) established in June 1890 by late His Highness The Maharaja Sayajirao Gaekwad III of Baroda State. Initially the idea was to teach drawing, bleaching, dyeing, calico printing and carpentry and there is a full-fledged workshop also located on the back side of the building there.

Being elected as FR made me widely known to students of all faculties of the university. My clean image and helpful nature were slowly taking the shape of a higher quality of love for humanity.

Prof. SS Merh was MS University Vice Chancellor and Prof. PJ Madan was Pro-Vice Chancellor.

Whenever any dispute arose either among the students or faculties or a reconciliation was required in any students related issue, the bigwigs of university looked for me. My friendly approach in such matters always helped. I could develop a rapport with VC and Pro-VC due to this. Also, I came to personally know all deans of various faculties too as they were chairpersons of various committees at university level.

Ambitions grew with passing of the years. There was even a time when I considered entering politics and become a Member of Parliament too! If that was not enough, I used to imagine myself as Cabinet Minister with portfolio of Ministry of Chemicals & Fertilizers! I soon realized that to go on compromising and all the inhuman traits a person needed to survive there was not my cup of tea and so I had dropped the idea before this bug could bit me more!

However, in 3rd year of B. Pharm, I contested the highest election at university level, that of MS University Staff & Students' Union Vice President, President of the Union being a nominated post by the State Government. A friend Nilesh Shukla was contesting for the same post too opposite me. We became temporary rivals during election!

I had planned a unique strategy to gain student votes. For filing nomination, a token fees of Rs.100 was to be paid by a candidate.

During my election campaign in university, I would urge the crowd: "Friends, I have no money to spend either on my publicity or to pay my nomination fees of Rs.100. If elected, I am going to work for you all. I guarantee that any kind of bungling will not happen during my tenure. If you trust me, I request you that please donate only 10 paisa (one tenth of a rupee) per student to pay for my deposit"

It was a simple strategy that those who would donate for me would also vote for me!

"If Taj Mahal Stands for its Beauty,

Chhabra Stands for his Duty!"

These lines used to be my opening and closing lines during election speeches!

Nilesh had a solid backing of Sanat Mehta who was Cabinet Minister for Finance of Gujarat State. Press media was fed with a story on previous day of our election with title: "Clear victory visible of Nilesh Shukla in University VP elections". On election day too, lot of rigging of votes took place and Nilesh won.

I lost by a meagre margin of just 325 votes!

I was learning to take things in my stride now. I had started looking at the brighter side of so called 'negative' events and was learning to deal with them as God's wish.

And God's wish knocked at my hostel room door in few days after the elections.

"*Sat Sri Akaal* Chhabra! How are you?"

I found CS Sitara Sir, Chief Instructor of Naval Wing of our NCC Unit standing at the door and greeting me.

"*Sat Sri Akaal Sirji....* please come in" I hurriedly started making my shabby hostel bed tidy and brought a chair for him.

"Will you go to Canada?" he directly asked me without any preface.

I did not know how to react and was fumbling for words.

"Look son, there is an Indo-Canada Youth Exchange Programme announced by the Central Government. There will be a selection process at national level for sending a group of talented young boys and girls to Canada under this programme. Favours and influences will be used from all quarters to get their own candidates included in the group. From MS University, you have been selected as our candidate. Now come fast to NCC Unit and start preparations."

Great Opportunity had knocked my door indeed.

In the national level selection, I got 5th rank. Our group had the opportunity to meet the then Prime Minister Mrs Indira Gandhi before leaving for Canada.

Sitting on the window seat of my flight to Canada, I felt as if my life had suddenly taken off to fly higher now.

Could this have been possible if I won VP election? Obviously not.

Whatever happens, happens for the best.

I never forgot this learning from my mother. She always used to add a quote, a line from Gurumukhi prayer, after saying it : *Sarbat da bhala!* Meaning that may the well-being prevail in the whole universe.

Destiny was now taking out its cards one by one from its magic hat!

If Taj Mahal Stands for its Beauty, Chhabra Stands for his Duty!

Chhabra was on duty assigned by God to him.

6.

Dream Enormously Big – Progress Knows No Bounds

> *Shoot for the moon. Even if you miss, you will land among the stars.*

My rich experience of six months as a part of the team sent under Indo-Canadian Youth Exchange Programme by the Govt of India strengthened my desire to start my own pharmaceutical company in future.

I was given an assignment with a Canadian company Trophic Canada Limited who were manufacturing natural nutritional supplements. Dr. Pandey was its CEO and under his able guidance, I successfully completed my assignment. The company was in Penticton, British Columbia State, Canada.

I was offered to work in Canada but I was determined to start my own business in India after completion of my studies.

"Sir, I have come to express my thanks and regards for my selection under Indo-Canadian Youth Exchange

Programme by the university" Upon return to India, I was seated in the chamber of MS University Vice Chancellor Prof. PJ Madan who was recently promoted to VC's position. My relations were extremely cordial with Prof. Madan and he always showered love whenever I met him.

"My studies have suffered due to this and it is going to be difficult for me to pass my final exams" I was worried.

Did I see God smiling again? Perhaps yes.

"Have you missed filling the form for mass promotion Chhabra?" Prof. Madan looked at me, surprised.

"Mass promotion!" "Sir I have no idea about it at all" I expressed my ignorance.

When I was in Canada, in 1981 students in Gujarat were agitating against the seat reservation policy of the government in various disciplines across the Gujarat. This agitation had stretched too long bringing the education at universities to a standstill. Hence, in that particular year government had announced that there will be no exams and all the students who wanted to carry on the studies next year were required to fill up the mass promotion option form.

The date for filling this form had lapsed long back.

Prof. Madan called his assistant and asked for a blank mass promotion form. He got it filled by me and assured not to worry. He would condone my late submission under his authority.

Now I realised why I saw God smiling. I was elated.

Yashoda!

When I was in KG, I fell deeply in love with one of our teachers, Jayshree Patel! Yes, I had crush over her as a child! Those who have not experienced this will find it difficult to digest, but this is a fact that children do have such infatuations.

During my college years, I experienced same love again for Yashoda Parmar, my classmate. She was a topper in the class. Yashoda was beautiful daughter of Indian father and German mother. From the day I knew her, I found her very pretty and also very balanced. While I was a student leader, she was academic leader!

In Third Year of Pharmacy, that being the last year and the last chance before anyone else proposed her, I decided to propose her. She used to stay just opposite to MS University Pavilion Ground and I requested her that I wanted to meet her at the Pavilion Ground the next day at 4.00 pm.

Yashoda came. Without much beating around the bush, I told her about my feelings for her and straightway proposed her. She listened quietly and said: "OK Chhabra! I will consult my mom. Is it ok with you if I reply you tomorrow here itself?"

"Absolutely fine with me Yashoda. I will be too happy if you reply in affirmative." I said.

She did return the next day but with non-affirmative reply.

"Sorry Chhabra, I talked to my mom. She said boys of this young age are just attracted to young girls. There is no need for you to go ahead in this matter."

"Oh, I see. Fine, Yashoda! All the best!" we departed at that.

That was my only proposal. That too declined!

I passed my final year exams without any crafts or jugglery during exams and got my Bachelor of Pharmacy degree from prestigious MS University of Baroda.

Soon after graduating, it was time to bid farewell to my dear MS University and to Vadodara City where I had received so much love and affection from one and all.

Cut to Jaipur! Pink City of India!

When I returned to my family at Jaipur, one thing was certain in my mind: clarity of my goal that I will anyhow start my own pharmaceutical company one day.

This characteristic – clarity in mind, has most of the time helped me achieve the desired goals in life.

Whenever I wrote something, I would start with a sentence which I had coined:

Progress Knows No Bounds

Later in life, when progress started, I used to write:

If I don't Get the Way, I will Make One

I did want to start my own company but there was no money available for it. Here, I followed one more belief system:

To succeed, Money is not Primary. Your Determination comes First.

If your desire is strong, you *will* find the way. I had complete faith in this saying and believe me, at that time I had yet not read "The Secret" by Rhonda Byrne.

Next ingredient necessary for starting a company was 'experience'. No one in my service class family had it.

To gain some experience in the pharma field, I decided to join service. I set a goal of 5 years by which I must leave the job and start my own business.

My job search began in Jaipur. One day, I went to see a friend Paramjeet Singh working with Punjab & Sind Bank. He took me for tea outside his branch to a *chai lari.*

Sipping the tea, suddenly, I saw a board on opposite side of the road and leaving the half cup of tea told Paramjeet "Yaar, please wait, I will just be back"

What I had seen was the sign board of the famous multinational pharma company "Sandoz India Limited!"

I went inside their office on ground floor.

"Yes gentleman! What can I do for you?" I was greeted by Branch Admin Manager Mr. VK Mehta.

"Sir, I have come here to find out if your company has any vacancy for the post of Medical Representative" I told Mr. Mehta.

"Fine. But I look after Admin here. For your enquiry, you should meet our Regional Manager Capt. Chopra whose cabin is on mezzanine floor" Mr. Mehta informed.

I hurriedly climbed the steps and located Capt. Chopra's cabin.

Capt. Chopra was a well-built, tall Punjabi Ex-Army Captain.

Without a blink of my eye, I blurted out what I had crammed while climbing the steps "Is that Captain Chopra? Sir, I have come here to find out if there is a vacancy of MR here. I am awaiting the results of my B. Pharm examination and I would like to apply"

Capt. Chopra listened patiently. "Look my boy! We don't have a vacancy at present" "But it will be there soon as somebody has resigned" He was kind enough to add. "You may apply as and when our ad appears in the newspapers"

The ad did appear in newspapers. I promptly applied.

Capt. Chopra was again there for the interview! Once done with routine questions, he shot a direct question "Tell us, why should we select you?"

"Sir, I have set a goal of 5 years for myself for progress. So, I am in a hurry to fulfil my own commitment. I will work day and night for quick success which will benefit both me and my company where I work" I candidly declared.

Capt. Chopra was impressed with my frankness. He selected me.

22nd August, 1982 was the joining date of my first job with Sandoz and hence, my self-set goal to become an entrepreneur would be 22nd August, 1987!

My career started and I learnt the job well in short span. One more twist in the offing! *God was still smiling!*

After few months, Capt. Chopra called me to his cabin and asked whether I would be comfortable to work from Udaipur. Ravindra Puri belonging to Jaipur wanted someone who would agree for mutual transfer as his entire family was at Jaipur. As I was a bachelor yet, he did not see any reason why I should not agree.

My mind started thinking quickly. Udaipur did have an air of fascination for me. Moreover, by the age of 25, I must marry and if I stay away from joint family, I will have time and space for emotional bonding with my spouse. Planning for kids was also necessary as one should settle them before retirement.

Considering all these, I agreed and shifted to Udaipur.

At Udaipur, I started working tirelessly. Colleagues called me workaholic.

And for one product of the company, I created history. Sandoz had manufactured a new analgesic called 'Optalidon." This drug proved to be a disaster at most places in Rajasthan except Udaipur. Udaipur territory was number one in sales of Optalidon.

How was this possible? **Belief system.**

I have always believed that faith can move mountains. I believed in the drug, had great faith in it and I proved the same to medical fraternity.

I never hesitated to visit doctors at Govt Hospitals even during midnight hours when they would be on night duty. Govt Hospitals at Rajasthan are very well-managed hospitals unlike at many other places. Company also recognised my sincerity and rewarded me with very good salary and incentives.

Here, the strategy was something like driving a vehicle at full speed and then leave it to run without accelerating, on its momentum. I had secured the market for my company so well that if I don't work so hard now, the sales will continue with that momentum effect. Otherwise also, I was doing the job just for the sake of getting experience. It was just the means, not goal.

Now was the correct time to marry. I slowed down the pace of my work. The sales would surely continue by the push of momentum I had created and even if they would slow down, blame was never to come on me as I had created the reputation of a most sincere MR.

I married a beautiful Punjabi girl from Indore with the same name as me, Kawaljeet. It was arranged marriage but it was love at first sight too! I call this period of our life as our 'longest honeymoon' period at Udaipur!

In the midst of such a glorious career in such a short span, I decided that I must now raise my status.

"Sir! I want to become an Area Manager." I was visiting my family in Jaipur and went to see our Regional Manager Capt. Chopra.

I will never forget the scene how Capt. Chopra burst out laughing and would not stop.

When he did, his words were: "Chhabra, you are too young to smoke! Understand this, there are 50 senior people in queue awaiting their promotion as Area

Manager. Continue doing your work sincerely and forget about promotion at this time"

I politely retorted back "Sir, I appreciate that there are seniors before me awaiting their promotion. But I will remember your uproarious laughter. I shall achieve what I have dreamt. Soon you will see your young Chhabra as an Area Manager."

I soon started applying to reputed multinational companies but due to lack of enough work experience, I was not found eligible.

Hence, I lowered my standards of companies and got selected as an Area Manager, Rajasthan by a company Bombay Tablets Manufacturing Company. Their HO was at Mumbai and my joining formalities were to be done there.

The moment I reached their office located at Princess Street, my heart sank seeing their small premises. *This was certainly not my dream office.*

I cannot work with this company. I declared my decision to myself there itself.

Immediately, I started hunting for Area Manager's job elsewhere. Soon, I got selected by a company Concept Pharmaceuticals Pvt Ltd, a sister concern of Lupin, as Area Manager, Rajasthan posted at Jaipur.

Here, for joining formalities I was required to go to Delhi at their headquarters.

Yet another twist in life was coming as I felt God smiling again.

31st October, 1984.

I was by birth a Sikh and used to keep beard and wear head turban. I never liked both. Once I had tried to get rid of it unilaterally and my father had coaxed me to re-enter into my Sardar *avtar*!

I left for Delhi to complete my joining formalities at Concept Pharma by Chetak Express from Jaipur. When it reached Delhi, what I witnessed was tragically shocking. Doctors, paramedics, stretchers, blood, lots of injured people and some dead too – all Sikhs, were all over the railway platform. Cries of anger, urgency, helplessness were mixed with a feeling of danger all around.

What had happened? When I tried to ask people, all of them looked at me with surprise.

Someone said "Hey *Sardarji*, you came by Chetak Express? How on earth you survived? There were attacks on Sikhs travelling by Chetak Express at Alwar and this is what happened. Rioters are taking revenge of our PM's murder today by attacking Sikhs everywhere."

OMG! I had heard the news in the afternoon before leaving by train but had never anticipated such brutal reaction.

Indian Prime Minister Indira Gandhi was assassinated at 9:29 a.m. on 31 October 1984 at her residence. She was killed by her Sikh bodyguards Satwant Singh and Beant Singh in the aftermath of Operation Blue Star. Operation Blue Star was an Indian military action carried out between 1 and 8 June 1984, ordered by Indira Gandhi to remove Jarnail Singh Bhindranwale and his followers from the holy Golden temple of the Harmandir Sahib in Amritsar, Punjab.

As a revengeful act against the whole Sikh community, anti-Sikh riots started, especially in Northern parts of India and thousands of people lost their lives in the massacre that followed.

Delhi was burning.

I immediately left the railway station and started looking for a rickshaw. One rickshaw wala became ready to drop me at my destination, Nirankari Colony at my own risk. I had no alternative but to take the risk.

Sitting in rickshaw, my contact was established, with Him!

Bhagwanji, you go on saving my life and you definitely have got great plans for me in life ahead. Fine. Thank You Bhagwanji!

Upon reaching safely at my destination, I got my hair cut short, became clean shaven and got rid of my 'sardar' identities for safety of my life.

New company in my new *avtar* awaited me!

Progress knows no bounds!

7.

Deh Shiva Bar Mohe Ihey, Shubh Karman Te Kabahu Na Taron!

> *"O Lord Shiva! Grant me this boon to never shirk from doing right."*

This war song of Sikhs has inspired me at each righteous step I have taken, may it be for welfare of self and family or for the society at large. This *Shabad* (hymn) was written in 17th Century by 10th Guru Gobind Singhji and is the religious anthem of Sikhs.

My job as Area Manager with Concept Pharma proved to be of my choice. I worked very hard and everything was in place as I settled quickly. But here too, I never allowed the comfort zones that came with the job to overlook my ambition: to start my own company. Job was just to get the managerial experience.

Once I quickly proved myself fit for the position I was given, I approached the management with a request to promote me to the post of Regional Manager or Product Executive at HO. Reply came similar to Sandoz: Experience of one and half year as MR and less than one year as Area Manager is not sufficient for the post of RM. Your demand is unrealistic and cannot be accepted.

Now?

Determination. This was not just a word for me. It was going to be my life mantra.

My self-set goal of spending only 5 years in job was closing in. With slightly more than two years left now when my Five-Year Plan will end, I started applying in large companies for the post of Product Executive. I received two offers: one from US Vitamins, Mumbai and another from Ranbaxy Laboratories, Delhi.

First, I went to Mumbai. When I was introduced to MD of US Vitamins, he asked me only few penetrating questions and instantly knew that I may not stay with the company for long. "You have selected a wrong candidate" He categorically declared to the HR Head of the company. "He shall use use our company as a stepping-stone. He is too ambitious."

The offer of Ranbaxy was already there. Ranbaxy's offer was strange. I was selected as Product Executive but to work in field for two years with my Head Office at Delhi. This was not suitable to me where touring from one place to another could be a great obstacle in planning for my now-nearing goal.

Here again, I played a gamble.

I had meanwhile got admission in evening course of MBA from Bhartiya Vidya Bhawans which I later on completed.

I thought of trying my hand in a different sales-field – selling photocopiers. A big name, Modi Xerox wanted Major Accounts (Sales) Manager for their Jaipur branch and I got selected.

Attractive pay package, perks and other benefits were given to me by the company and I could not ask for more.

But here was the trap which, if ignored, could have never let me go ahead.

I pondered over and over and took a strange looking decision. In the midst of my job's superb comfort zone, much before the arrival of 1987, I decided to quit.

Once decided, why wait? Deh Shiva Bar Mohe!

So, one fine morning I prepared my resignation letter and put it on the table of Shri Ashok Wadhawan, my boss at Modi Xerox.

"Hey Chhabra! What is this? You got a better offer or what?" He looked surprised.

"No Sir. I want to start my own company" I said. Coolly.

When I returned home and declared that I had left the job, there was a wave of shock in the family. Neither my father nor anybody in the family had any business experience. The family had no such resources that it could support me to start my own company. By this time, we already had our first daughter Namrata (Sweety) and without my earning support, my drastic decision looked very unfavourable to the whole family.

A book by Napoleon Hill "Think and Grow Rich" was my inspiration. In this book, Law of Success is powerfully summarized. He has explained in the book that when you must take great risks to achieve bigger goals, ask yourself these questions:

1. If I do something and if I don't succeed, am I going to lose my life?

My answer to this question was: No

2. What is the worst that can happen? Are all your investments going to be wasted?

My answer to this question was: I have nothing! Where is anything to lose? I have not yet begun and not invested anything at all. Hence, no question of any loss.

I had thought about the first question too that if I fail miserably in business, I had my option ready to start doing a job again, may be with few compromises here and there. But if this is the price I have to pay against what I might achieve in business, then it was worth it!

One more important aspect of my decision would be my wife. If I failed, Kawaljeet who came from a business family would be most affected person.

But suddenly I realized that God was smiling from the corner of his lips this time. Kawaljeet from her young age has been extremely bold and enterprising. Always encouraging me to scale greater heights.

In her usual calm, composed, collected manner she said: "Take a plunge! Come what may!"

And I jumped!

Money was the immediate need to start anything. I did not want to borrow any money from the family. All that I had earned were spent in honeymoon and outings.

"Come on KS! What is your strength?" I asked myself.

They were many.

I was by now quite conversant with job market. I had developed quite a few knacks like how to prepare a great profile, how to crack exams, how to succeed in an interview, when to switch job, what are the avenues for getting a rise and such other strategies related to job market.

I started a Training Institute at our home itself. My offer to students and clients was also lucrative: Pay only if you succeed. Pay what? Your one month's salary.

Individuals, Executives, Senior Managers from reputed companies became my clients. This was just a stop-gap arrangement because sitting at home, I started planning for my own pharma business.

First step was to get a Wholesale Drug License. I had to print few stationary and show some office furniture also.

But where was the money for license fee and for bribe to Drug Inspector?

Kawaljeet offered to sell off her gold received in marriage worth Rs.3500 for the license fee. I paid the fee and on personal meeting with Drug Inspector, frankly told him my life story. I clearly told him that I had no money to offer to him for getting my license.

Drug Inspector obliged.

After receiving the license, my own company, although still on paper only, was formed : Health Care Formulations Pvt Ltd!

My father had taken a promise from me that whenever I start my own company, I will keep my younger brother Paramvir with me in business.

I kept my promise. While I became the Managing Director, I included Kawaljeet and Paramvir both as Directors in the company.

Next million-dollar question was: how do we get the products? There was no money to buy raw material and manufacture them.

Many of my classmates had started their own small-scale industries by this time. As I had maintained strong relations even after leaving the studies with them. Shailesh Choksi of "Shaimil Laboratories" and Vipul Shah of "Akshar Pharmaceuticals" without any hesitation agreed to make products for us on credit.

The company was launched at Jaipur. As we could not afford employing any Medical Representatives, me and Paramvir acted as Medical Representatives but we made designations for us as Regional Manager and Area Manager respectively!

"RM and Area Managers are themselves here to sell products?" clients would ask. We had a story to tell them that this product is such that its first launching has to be done by RM and Area Manager themselves!

We both worked really hard and slowly the business picked up. In fact, it started growing. It was now becoming difficult for us to meet the demands in time. Short supply of product soon started. Because of their own work pressures, both my friends found it difficult to maintain the delivery schedules of product too.

We took a decision to shift to Vadodara with our daughter Namrata.

We took a rented room which was "all-in-one" – a bathroom, a kitchen, drawing room and bedroom – all in one room!! Rent was Rs.425 per month. This was in year 1988.

Shifting to Vadodara to get the products in time didn't help. The situation soon started worsening and our monetary condition became pathetic. My readers may find it difficult to digest but we really faced very tough times.

There was a time when we could not afford even a 1 Rupee balloon for our daughter as only Rs.10 were left in balance and three days to go before I get some more money.

I never let my father know about it but he somehow sensed it and one day suddenly landed at Vadodara.

Seeing our pitiable condition, my father broke down.

"*Kya haal kar diya hai meri beti ka tune Kawal?*" he could barely complete his sentence and started crying.

"Look son, we have no dearth of food and shelter. Stop this nonsensical drama of business, come back to Jaipur and re-start your job." His words were a typical mix of authority and earnest appeal.

Stubborn kind of fighting spirit may or may not fetch the desired results all the time.

But I, being I, was not the one to back out so easily.

I had great faith in Guru Gobind Singhji's war song *Deh Shiva Bar Mohe Ihe, Shubh Karman Te kabahu Na Taron!*

I will not back out. No way.

My greatest quality was at its peak now:

Determination.

8.

The Art of Risking

> *Risk is the only guarantee to be truly alive!*
>
> *Osho*

If strong willpower and determination are combined with passion, a path that seems non-existent is created. Your perseverance and mettle to cope with risks will work like magic.

A deep trust that the whole universe is there to help you climb great heights is needed.

These words are coming from my own struggle, my real-life experiences, the agonies that I passed through. No pain, no gain!

The 'magic' worked. Soon, the sales picked up and Paramvir started sending money to us from Jaipur.

"Win the hearts of people in business too, as you have been doing all along your life. Waheguruji is with you." Even though leaving Vadodara with a heavy heart, father had blessed me.

True blessings always work. Golden words can change life.

Paradise lost was regained! Determination started reaping fruits. Within a short period, we shifted to Lucky Apartments near ONGC at Pratapnagar. Rent Rs.1300. Year was 1989.

Business started flourishing. So much that for expansion, we needed to have our headquarters at Vadodara. So, we took a tenement at Padam Park Society at Makarpura at rent of Rs.550.

This became the first office of Healthcare Formulations Pvt. Ltd. Kishor Solanki was our first employee! He is still there after 34 years!

In few years, Business started growing by leaps and bounds. We shifted our house to 10/A, Gokul Society on Sindhvai Mata Road at a rent of Rs.3500.

We added new products. Profits started soaring. A larger office with warehouse was required. In the same Gokul Society where we stayed, we took such facility on rent.

Premiums were offered for our products although they were costlier than others.

Why?

Apart from selling products, we offered our customers value added services like giving them guidelines to promote their sales, sharing with them market strategies etc.

One can succeed anywhere in any field if we carry the purest of intentions and helpful attitude in our heart. Cheating humans is easy, but cheating Him is impossible.

Life had taken a huge turn.

From struggle and deprivations to comfort and abundance.

In 1990, our second daughter Amrit was born.

Paramvir was now of marriageable age. As I had promised my father that I will always look after him, I did not want him to receive half share when business segregation happens in future. He must own it whole. Slowly I started working in that direction. I started making him independent but did not let him know what was going in my mind.

Yet another bold decision was taken.

In 1990, I transferred my well-established, flourished company Healthcare Formulations Pvt. Ltd. in Paramvir's name.

In the same year, I formed a new proprietorship business for myself: Hindustan Pharmaceuticals.

One more risk!

I have always been fascinated by what Osho has said about risk:

Remember one thing: never forget the art of risking, never, never. Always remain capable of risking. And wherever you can find an opportunity to risk, never miss it, and you will never be a loser. Risk is the only guarantee to be truly alive.

Hindustan Pharma was the tiniest unit one could imagine! At the inauguration function, MD of a famous pharma company sarcastically remarked: "*Chhabra, Ye kya kabutarkhana banaya hai tumne?*"

Business was zero and liabilities of loans from various institutions, banks, individuals etc. were enormous. Incidentally, the first business loan we took was for Rs.25000 from State Bank of India, Jaipur.

Slacklining or art of balancing while walking on a rope requires huge focus, a cool mind and trust in yourself. On rope called 'life,' perhaps, I had learnt this art by now.

I had complete trust in what I always used to say to myself: **If there is no way, I will make one.**

This time I had deliberately plunged into the unknown sea with my small boat knowing fully well that it may see the shore or perish.

The lyrics of famous Lata Mangeshkar song used to haunt me :

Kyun mai tufan se darun, mera sahil aap hai

And my *sahil,* my sea-shore, was God Himself!

My dialogues and one-to-one meetings with Him had never stopped in any situation.

He had blessed me with the greatest wealth of my life by this time.

Reputation.

Reputation in the society and business worked wonders for me. I had decided not to draw money from Healthcare. Nor I wanted to disturb my parents or my in-laws.

So, I borrowed. I could borrow as much as I needed as no friend or no institution hesitated in lending me any amount.

When I was doing my MBA from Bhawans at Jaipur, I used to regularly read one Singapore Publication "Executive Digest". There was one article by Peter Drucker whose writings contributed to the philosophical and practical foundations of the modern business which had one sentence which I never forgot: **"When in difficulty, think outside the box"**

In India, the businesses had started seeing mergers and acquisitions as the government had opened the doors for foreign companies. As a result, many capable and well experienced people had started living in fear of losing their jobs. Many had already lost and on others, the sword of retrenchment was hanging.

I saw an opportunity in this. Why not utilize their capabilities? A truly 'outside the box' thought emerged in my mind and I acted upon it.

Ad was given in Lucknow newspapers. I selected Lucknow because UP being the largest state of India, there are maximum number of well-experienced pharma managers and representatives who may be looking for alternative sources of earning. The ad contained lucrative offer for the people with uncertain future: "Are you a pharma professional with good selling capability but a victim of merger? Quit your jobs and become an independent businessman. You can earn 10 times than your salary. We shall help you to do so. No risk involved."

The response I got was astonishing. My ad had touched the unsatisfied need of those people.

People started contacting me and the pertinent question was: what about the money to be invested?

I offered them to invest their VRS money which will fetch them good profits once the business picked up.

Many of them showed interest and started investing. I accepted whatever came my way. From Rs.10,000 to Rs.3,00,000. I could help each and every one according to their investment start their independent business.

Within short time, I became quite a specialist in this. They got their products manufactured from us and started selling them with their brand names.

In a very short span, all those who invested in this manner started owning cars and many of them even became big shots.

We were now so much in demand that we had more business in hand than we could handle. We started to be selective. Although our products were costlier than others in the market, because of value added services like marketing strategies and methodology to sell their products, we succeeded.

A time came when our company was now considered one of the most well to do small sector pharma company across the State of Gujarat!

I started repaying all my loans and debts. Once again, paradise was regained.

I am tempted to quote a famous dialogue from a popular OTT series here:

"*Risk Hai to Ishq Hai!*"

Ishq in my case was always with Life itself!

9.

Stable and Able

The Stable and Able is second chapter of Shrimad Bhagwad Geeta where Arjun who sunk down in depression, was shaken up by the brilliance of light of self to stand up and to become awake. Arjun then recollects his intellect, mind, and body and reaches a stage of quest and inquiry.

Turning Towards Path of Enlightenment

"Stable and Able" is a book written by Guruji Shri G. Narayana, also known as "Management Guru" in corporate circles. This book, like mariner's compass can help anyone to navigate the dangerous sea of human life.

Guruji is an enlightened soul. Since our first meeting, I was attracted by his knowledge, his compassionate presence and his tremendous love for whosoever he came across. His teachings, blessings and love in abundance have always remained my greatest inspiration in good times as well as challenging times.

My company, Hindustan Pharmaceuticals had now received the reputation of one of the best Micro, Small & Medium Enterprises (MSME) in Gujarat. Our new unit was located at Por GIDC.

During those years, India was emerging as Pharmacy of The World. Countries from all over the world were sourcing their pharmaceutical needs from India. This was because of less cost of manufacturing and still good quality of drugs. It was predicted in many studies that India will lead the world in pharma in next 10 years. It was indeed going to be a 'sunrise industry' soon.

If such golden opportunities were in the offing, our Company too had to be ready for it.

How?

Let us make our company a cutting-edge, world-class company!

Not a small step but a huge leap would be required to achieve this goal.

"Good Manufacturing Practices" (WHO-cGMP) certification from World Health Organisation was a sure shot to sky-rocket your company at that time.

At least Rs.4 to 5 crores were required to make Hindustan Pharma a world class company! Because the process would entail a complete upgradation of manufacturing facilities and total facelift of the facility so as to meet the norms set by WHO.

As our business was a well-established one and the reputation that we had earned was our biggest strength, we could easily borrow whatever amount of money needed.

We literally went on a borrowing spree because all our profits were being invested in business only. Hence, there was no liquidity. From whichever source possible, may it be bank, financial institutions, individuals – everywhere, we borrowed and collected the amount needed.

Yet another risk! My permanent companion, *Bhagwanji* seemed silently watching as if letting me play in whichever way I wanted and face come-what-may situation!

The goal was achieved ultimately. We could make our company a top-class company fit for WHO-cGMP certification.

The certificate of compliance by WHO-cGMP was granted to Hindustan Pharma!

In Gujarat, the company became a role model Pharma MSME company. We had hired top-notch consultants and best of the employees too to maintain the raised standards.

But the irony was that the unit was a top unit with top liabilities!

I do go on wondering how and why on earth was this game of 'paradise lost' and 'paradise regained' continuously going on in my life?

I never thought, in my wildest dreams, that one more time the destiny was going to be cruel and all my efforts, labour, passion would crash like house of cards.

Yet one more tsunami hit the now settled calm waters of our life.

In 1995, during the regime of the then PM Shri PV Narsimha Rao, Central Government took some drastic decisions to regulate drug prices and their manufacturing practices which gave an earthquake like jolt to the entire pharma industry, more particularly to the MSME sector.

First blow was the Drugs Price Control Order (DPCO). Before this order, there was no governmental control over the prices of drugs and manufacturers could sell their products at will. This meant that medicines with similar base drugs were having huge variations in their market price. Government was of the view that pharma industry is minting money in this manner and the general public is the sufferer. In a way this was true also.

Under this order, all drug manufacturers were required to submit the costing of the drug on the basis of which government would decide its permissible MRP.

This was the first heavy blow on our business which was a role model and a world class company now.

Second blow was soon to come.

We were paying Central Excise duty on first clearance value till now. Government ruled that this will be applicable on selling price henceforth. This resulted in a sharp increase of duty by10 times more, in many cases.

Entire pharmaceutical industry in the country was shaken up. Profits started declining and many units were on the verge of closure due to these policy changes of the government.

Final 'death nail' on the coffin of pharma industry was put by the government with declaring some States like Himachal Pradesh, J&K, Sikkim as "Central Excise Free Zones."

Huge set-back in pharma industry started. Profits declined to their lowest. Many units closed down. Thousands became jobless. Big companies shifted their manufacturing facilities to Excise Free Zones.

An atmosphere of total dismay prevailed in pharma circles because of the U-turn in government policy.

I always believed that I had found the niche in the pharma market, especially a unique speciality in 'third party manufacturing.' But with the new policy, our products became 40% more costlier than our competitors who had started manufacturing from the above States.

In a period of just six months, 90% of our clients left us and started sourcing their needs from States having Excise Free Zones. Obviously because of less price.

The tsunami had to come when me and my family had started seeing the glory of best of the materialistic happiness.

We had one of the finest bungalows in the city and Times of India had specially carried an article on it.

Our car was imported Corolla with chauffer always in spic and span white uniform with cap!

Manufacturing facilities were top class. My own chamber was state-of-the-art kind which would match with those in topmost corporates.

It quickly washed away everything I had dreamt of and achieved in life.

Crores of rupees were borrowed to be repaid from future profits, whereas profit had now become zero. Although there were no losses, the liquidity was not there.

There was no liquid money to pay EMIs to financial institutions or private individuals. Repayment defaults started very soon. Going by my clean reputation, the demands for money repayments were extremely difficult for me to handle.

In no time, our company was on the verge of closure any moment. I stopped sharing my frustration with Kawal.

For the first time in life, my communication with God was disrupted. Connection was lost. I started groping in total dark in absence of His light.

My self-confidence evaporated in thin air. I had completely broken down.

Sleep evaded me. When it came due to fatigue, I had nightmares.

This was too much to bear.

Suicide. Yes. Suicide is the solution.

I started hearing these words inside me as if coming from far distance. My own voice sounded strange but I was mesmerised by it. Negative forces can also have a kind of magnetic pull if you fall prey to them.

And I was hypnotised by my own self-suggestions going on inside me day in, day out.

They say you require tremendous courage to commit suicide. People with great courage only can take a decision to end life.

This will sound contrary to normal belief that such people are cowards, but I can vouch for this that it does require enormous courage to commit suicide.

Enough is enough. I will end my life tomorrow.

I took the final decision.

Next day, around 11.30 am, without telling anything to anybody, I left my office in my car. I had decided to jump on Railway tracks at the time of a super-fast train passing by Vishwamaitri Bridge near Kalali.

When I reached in my car near Manisha Chowkdi on OP Road, I could not resist to have last *darshan* of Guruji before leaving this world.

I rang him. Usually, he would not be at home at this time of the day, but that day he himself picked up the phone. He was at home as his flight from Hyderabad was delayed and he had to postpone his other engagements at Vadodara.

"Yes, Chhabraji" Guruji's compassionate voice created unexplainable ripples in my heart.

"Guruji, *milna hai*" My voice trailed speaking such short sentence also.

"Come right away" Guruji said, perhaps sensing something unusual in my voice.

I drove towards his residence.

Guruji was sitting in his drawing room. Cool, calm, collected as always.

The moment Guruji looked at me with his ever-pervading kind looks in the eyes and smiling face and asked in his loving manner: "*Kaise ho Chhabraji? Kya Chalta Hai*?" a huge wave of pent-up emotions stirred the ocean of tears accumulated at the bottom of my heart.

I started sobbing uncontrollably instead of replying. He took me in his arms trying to provide solace.

I must have cried in Guruji's arms for at least half an hour.

Guruji lovingly cuddled me, patted on my back and asked softly:

"What has happened? Is your wife alright? Kids ok?"

"Yes, they are all fine Guruji" I replied, still in a choked voice.

"Then? What's the problem?"

"Huge losses in business. Debts. Repayment defaults. I am broke" I stuttered.

"Hmm." He listened. Unmoved. Silently. "So, what is your plan?" Guruji asked a pointed question looking straight in my eyes.

"Suicide" I stubbornly replied, looking the other way ignoring his penetrating eyes.

Guruji's reaction was astonishing!

"Fine!" He said: "We will plan your suicide. But there is a condition. First you take this book from me, read it and then come back. We will find out easy ways of committing suicide for you!"

I looked at him, puzzled, for some moments. Then I realised his trick. He had allowed my weak moments to pass.

That book was the one I have referred at the beginning of this chapter, "Stable and Able" which is written by him. In the book, Guruji has explained beautifully what Lord Krishna explained Arjun in Shrimad Bhagwad Geeta about *sthitpragyata,* how a person of steady wisdom, the stable one, can tackle different situations in life with equal tranquil state of mind as he has realised the truth from within.

The catharsis of weeping incessantly and Guruji's calm vibes washed away all the negativities from the innermost core of my being.

During those unforgettable moments with him, I experienced the peace which I had known never before. A hurricane of negative forces had passed by me and I had survived the storm one more time.

God was smiling once again with all His glory in the bright, clear, spotless sky of my inner world.

I bowed my head, touched Guruji's feet and promised him to ride over my weak moments.

A great spiritual beginning was made. Beginning of one of the greatest learnings in spiritual world: *Sthitpragyata.*

I never knew that this incident will bring the ultimate turning point in my life. It was as if my mind was illuminated. I had clear vision now. No confusion, no negativity, just the inner bliss prevailed. It was home-coming.

Thank you Guruji! You are the divine blessing, the enlightening angel in my life.

I had a glimpse of how it felt to be Stable.

I once again needed to be Able.

10.

Rise and Recharge

> *"Stand up, be bold, and take the blame on your own shoulders. Do not go about throwing mud at others; for all the faults you suffer from, you are the sole and only cause."*
>
> *-Swami Vivekanand.*

There is a large hoarding placed outside Vivekanand Kendra on Alkapuri Road of Vadodara city of the world-famous picture of Swami Vivekanand.

I must have passed it thousand times before. After reading the small book given by Guruji, it suddenly dawned on me that Swamiji's picture was a perfect example of *sthitpragyata* personified! If we just visualise it while facing any unusual situation, good or bad, we regain our balance of mind.

This is one of my very important messages that if one can stay steadfast in any kind of situation, no seemingly adverse condition will be able to touch the very core of your being.

The art of staying unmoved by external situations is, of course, a tough art to learn; but by practice, we can master it to a great extent. Once we learn it, the anguish in life vanishes.

Nothing in life is permanent and change is inevitable.

It took me three days to complete the reading of that small book. The book was small but atomic.

It opened my mind to understand the reality that whatever happens in our life is the sum result of our own deeds. If I fell head on, it was my sole responsibility as I must have indulged myself in the blind-race to achieve some extra material gains. My family had always stood in my support and I had no right to punish them with the sufferings that would follow if I committed suicide.

How could I be so selfish?

Some thoughts, some sentences in the book which applied to my situation, stimulated my mind. *Worrying will not help in any manner. Adverse situations are reversible. Just start taking corrective actions and they will improve. Only you know where you are stranded. Try to come out of it and slowly slowly, you will come out. Nothing is permanent here, neither unhappiness, nor happiness.*

Face the challenge!

Rise!

Revive!

Connection with Almighty which seemed disrupted started re-establishing. Inclination towards spirituality was much more now than ever.

Although, huge amounts were outstanding to be paid to debtors, a certain tranquillity in heart prevailed.

Silence after storm! Perhaps storms don't come to teach us painful lessons, rather they were meant to wash us clean!

The kind of storm that hit my life had uprooted, with many other things, the negative thoughts too.

A silent mind gets newer ideas as it can now see the forward path with clarity.

Can I start something new which will take me out of this pathetic looking situation? I started pondering over this thought and soon I found a way out.

"Outside The Box" thinking helped here too!

We formed a new company: Hindustan Biosynth Limited, this time with manufacturing of herbal products.

Workers in the company also were confident that they will get their salaries once the business picks up. Without pay, they laboured day in, day out which resulted in sharp increase in productivity. Few of them did leave, but we took it as a reduced burden.

An adverse effect of this showed too. According to Drug Control Policy, you have to keep qualified people only in certain departments. We violated this rule. Here too, reputation did its magic. Drug Inspectors would visit our manufacturing facility but would overlook such violations without any expectation. Few offered help too!

On other hand, one favourable rule helped to revive the business. If yours was a new company and the turnover was up to a certain limit, the products were exempted from Central Excise Duty.

Taking advantage of this provision, we bifurcated my company from one company to five companies: Hindustan Pharmaceuticals, Hindustan Biosynth Ltd, Health & Hygiene Products India Ltd, Excel Grieves India Ltd and Excel Pharmachem Industries.

With this bifurcation, excise duty became zero!

Arijit Bhattacharya, our Sales Manager in Health & Hygiene Products India Ltd. had a fertile brain. He came up with the idea that we make distributors and take hefty deposits from them. In a good Delhi hotel, we organised walk-in interviews and could collect deposit amount of about Rs.10 lakhs. This was a huge amount for me in the times of need. One distributor, owner of Amar Medical Agency soon needed his money back as his father had expired and he also became broke. It took me some time to return his money.

A businessman from Delhi Anil Achantani who had taken distributorship for products of Hindustan Biosynth could not run his business and became bankrupt. He had purchased goods worth Rs.10 lakhs from us. He asked for his money to be returned. Now this was an extremely difficult proposition as money in business is always rotated as turnover. His sister was staying in Vadodara and through her he made continuous follow ups. Although it was difficult for me to meet his demand immediately, our relations started becoming strong. He and his sister both were assured of one fact that Chhabra will one day definitely return the amount.

Later, when I sold my business I called Anita, Anil's sister and handed over her whatever I could salvage out of his returned products which already had become scrap by now.

Anita Shivnani was going to have a more fruitful association with my endeavours in serving the humanity in future.

Interestingly, by this time, the products manufactured by the companies located in Excise Free Zone States had started getting bad reputation in the pharma market. Moreover, we were able to now sell those products at their rate at Vadodara itself too!

With unending grace of God, the company started doing very well soon. It quickly flourished into a profit-making company again. So much so that I was now able to start repayments of my loans.

Good old days soon returned!

Paradise was once again regained!

The Triumph of Integrity and Honesty.

What is important and inspiring here is one thing that we were very truthful to each person who lent us money. I never befooled anyone and frankly put forth my situation before them as it was.

I never went undercover from my moneylenders. Every time they would raise demands, I used to explain them my situation and pleaded them to have trust that once I regain my stability in business, my first priority would be to return their money. Some would ask for a target date and my answer would be that I have no idea about it but I always pray to God that please do not take me away in such situation where I may have to leave without repaying my debts. They would glance at me as if not much convinced by such dialogues.

There were also many kind hearted and understanding people who solaced me and told me not to worry.

Some angelic souls even went to the extent of assuring me even more financial help if needed! Such silver lining during the terrible period was unbelievable but true. All such true ambassadors of God were coincidentally from Jain community!

I had to tackle some unyielding types also. Also, there were some who threatened to kill me. I would tell them: "Please do it now! Although you all are such gentlemen, why don't you understand that this way you will lose the probable return of money."

Banks and financial institutions were generous too. Most of them restructured my loans with favourable modifications in EMIs. They appeared convinced by my argument that if the factory is closed down, they will not get anything back which they might if I bounced back in business.

Truthfulness, as they say, is the main element of character and is the foundation of all the virtues of mankind.

This quality really has worked wonders throughout in my life. People who lent money had lost patience but all the same, they were confident that as and when Chhabra regains his old glory, he will definitely return our money.

I can never forget BM Shah family, who are part of our own family. They often helped me financially in my business. Ansuya aunty and her husband Biharilal uncle never hesitated to lend me money even when I was broke. Their son Rajesh, my brother, and daughter Sonal, my sister, were quite fond of me. Sonal's talented daughter is Naomy who was in later years going to connect with me in service to humanity as an Architect!

God sends Angels to help me.

One morning, during my tough days when I was still struggling to stabilise my business and was yet not stable enough in mind, a gentleman in white kurta pyjama knocked my door. When I opened the door and looked in his eyes, I saw a familiar face.

"*Om Shanti*" he greeted me with folded hands and smiling face.

Later, I found out that it was their code of conduct to greet others in that manner.

He was a messenger from Brahma Kumaris.

"Chhabraji, on the day of Mahashivratri, we would like to lighten the lamp with your hands at our Centre. Please accept our invitation."

"Gentleman, it seems you have knocked the wrong door. I am perhaps not the person you are looking for" I bluntly told him although he had no idea about my broken-down condition.

"No Chhabraji! Didi has specifically written down your name and address on her card and given to me. Look" he flashed an invitation card from Brahma Kumari Meena Didi.

I looked at it, puzzled.

"You will have to come Sir!" the gentleman continued. "This is our address and we will look forward to meet you on Mahashivratri day. Om Shanti."

In life, God has sent countless angels to me. This gentleman was also an angel.

His name was Jitubhai Patel.

When I met Brahma Kumari Meena Didi, I frankly told her about my broken-down condition and expressed that in no way I am fit for gracing any such function.

"That's exactly why Baba has chosen you Chhabraji!" she said with a compassionate smile. "Lots of people have given your reference to us and now it is between you and Baba!"

Another angel!

This was where one more spiritual dimension opened up in my life. I started connecting with Baba in day-to-day dealings with people. In situations which I would feel were going out of my control, say if someone would upset me to the extent of getting irritated, I would request Baba to take over.

Baba definitely took over. At the end, the person who was irritated with me out of his own frustration, would leave happily, in a blissful state of mind. He may have come to recover his money from me, but would leave saying not to worry and go ahead in business.

This is how divine and positive forces in life start helping you. Through angels.

First, I thought me and Kawal were alone to face the world. Now I realised that the divinity is ever present. We just have to be open and allow it in.

Once we were out of the money crisis, I started paying serious attention to the inner voice which was now louder than ever.

There was now a philosophical turn in my thought process.

The thought that there must be millions suffering from such miserable situations in life would not allow me to rest.

This is exactly how my Affair with Humanity started!

The voice from within. Divinity flows...

Every night while going to sleep, a caravan of thoughts started haunting me. They were all self-questions.

What exactly is the purpose of life?

What exactly is God's will behind all these topsy turvy happenings in my life?

Why He drove me to a saturation point where I decided to commit suicide but could not?

If my paradise was lost again and again, why it always was regained every time?

Most importantly, why He saved my life so many times?

Birth with my sac intact, saved from huge stone-fall in childhood, saved from anti-Sikh riots in train, saved from the fatal car accident on the road and now saved from the suicide attempt.

Why? Oh Bhagwanji, why?

I searched for answers day in, day out.

I settled for the only convincing answer which dawned on me:

You are the chosen one from amongst many to take lead and serve the humanity for the rest of your life.

I shared my thoughts with Kawal and she, not even once resisted. It was her mettle, inspiration and spirit which had really provided me invaluable support in all adversities.

For sewa too, she became ready to support totally.

The seeds of serving the humanity were sown in our hearts.

God gifted me with a new slogan:

जो प्राप्त है, वह पर्याप्त है!

Counting money for the whole life is not going to give you real happiness. If you start giving, the joy of giving is all yours. If you engage yourself along with your resources in service to humanity, this very earth is heaven.

The time to be happy is 'now', the place to be happy is 'here', and the way to be happy is to make someone happy and create a little heaven 'right here'.

These simple looking nursery rhyme lyrics are pregnant with beautiful meaning.

It would be interesting for the readers to know how my resolution to enter into sewa-world transformed into pledge!

A movie and one of its central ideas were responsible for it!

The movie was "Three Idiots".

One of its central ideas was CHASE YOUR PASSION.

While coming out of the theatre, I had made up my mind not to think twice now to chase my sewa-passion.

The idea appealed to me so much that I soon started making efforts towards putting into practise what I wanted to do now.

First step towards helping the humanity was taken in 2010 by starting a Life Counselling Service from my residence. People started coming for guidance and solutions for their various issues. Some of the beneficiaries were from Vadodara's "who's who" too!

Initially, the inspiration from 'above' was: keep working and also keep helping others simultaneously.

Soon, the feeling gripped me that I must call it a day now. We have had enough and why not, with the help of well-wishers and friends, start a full-fledged registered NGO which will have a wide scope to reach thousands of underprivileged people.

This would require that we must sell-off my business for serving the humanity with total commitment.

It took about three years' time for me to find a good customer to sell my well-established profit-making company.

Ultimately, the business got sold on 30th September, 2013.

It was time now to serve the suffering humanity in every possible way – full time!

It was time to Rise and Recharge in a different dimension now, that of humanity.

I was now a liberated bird. A liberated soul!

To serve the humanity was the sole goal – here onwards.

A free flying bird!

11.

In Love with Humanity

> *Helping hands are better than praying lips. Do ordinary things with extraordinary love.*
>
> *– Mother Teresa*

In year 2010, we started social services like Life Counselling, Vastradan, Netradan and few others under the banner of "Anand Ashram" – Anand Ashram meaning where you get "Anand (bliss)!"

Since the day I renounced my flourished business at the age of 53, my heart has remained filled with compassion for the suffering humanity. Having been an achiever in pharma business, I always wanted to achieve great heights in social service too. My thinking always has been that of a visionary.

All that you need to do is : pursue your goals. Follow your passion. Success will be surely yours.

In 2012, Anand Ashram Charitable Trust was registered as an NGO. As the time passed, more and more talented people from different walks of life joined the sewa-brigade. More and more social services were added too.

Overwhelming response from near and dear ones started pouring in. It was indeed heartening to know that so many people wanted to do social service but were not able to find a proper platform. Compassion overflowed in hearts all around, a direction was required to channelise that flow.

During those initial days of social service, I was also passionately involved in revamping of Vadodara City crematoriums. Of course, the money came from the corporates but huge efforts to connect the dots were required for the project. Mukesh Ambani, India's No.1 industrialist also took interest in the project and had helped it financially too. The then Member of Parliament Jayaben Thakkar, Shri Jagdish Thakkar, Shri Amul Jikar, Shri Bharat Shah, Shri Ramesh Jatia, Shri Chetan Sandesara and the people of Vadodara made it possible in togetherness under the banner of Rotary Club of Baroda, Jawaharnagar.

New ideas started pouring in. Newer social services were added one after another. Donors regularly started donating money for the noble causes.

Anand Ashram Charitable Trust is now a leading NGO in Gujarat. It's various social services are: *Ashayein, Jeevan Mulya, Vidya Sahayog, Swa-Shakti, Vastradan, Raktdan, Netradan, Planet Protectors, My Green*

Vadodara, Sathi Hath Badhana, Senior Citizens Spiritual Sewa, Life Coaching, Career Counselling, Happiness Home for the Senior Citizens "Swarg". Readers interested to know in detail about these services may please visit the website *www.anandashram.ngo*

One touching incident happened when I was visiting a principal of one Municipal Primary School in connection with Anand Ashram's Jeevan Mulya service. I was sitting on a bench outside. It was recess time and little girls of primary school were playing in the lobby. The children got settled around me. To pass time creatively, I started asking them one by one what they intend to become in life when they grow up.

One girl said she would like to become police, another said doctor and someone even said prime minister!

But I was moved from the deepest core of my heart by one answer from an extremely needy looking girl. "Sir, my mother has told me that after I complete my education in school, there is no need to study further." The girl innocently informed me.

"Why?" I wanted to know from her.

"Sir, my father has expired and my mother is doing some domestic work and that is how our family is run. I will join her after my schooling and help her in work. We do not have money to pay college fees"

I was dumbfounded. Speechless. It was a heart stirring answer. Choked with emotions, I could not control my tears.

That night, sleep evaded me once again.

O God! If such is the scenario, how on earth my country's women will strengthen? How can I and my friends help improve such situations?

I was always advocating the idea of women empowerment. I had seen Kawal manage our business during my hospitalisation for long and I was proud of her strengths. But here was a live example how such empowerment is hampered for want of money. For want of fees to study further, girls drop out and either do domestic work or are married at early age.

Anand Ashram's flagship project: "Ashayein" was born that day!

I floated a touching message to my near and dear ones and desired that we start a social service under which we will support underprivileged girl students who have passed their 12th Std, but are not able to study further in university due to want of money. We can pay for their education till they graduate. Later, we can extend the support even for post-graduation and research.

By next day evening, money started depositing in Anand Ashram's bank account and to begin with, we were able to support 11 underprivileged girl students. This number kept on rising every year and this extremely important social service has grown significantly since then.

Having studied many cases of these needy girls, having seen them graduating and getting good jobs, having seen their happy, smiling faces when they visit Anand Ashram events, I am pretty sure this social service has far-reaching results in the society. I am humbled and sincerely thankful to Anand Ashram's donors, team members and all the volunteers and kind Corporates who have always extended support for this exemplary sewa.

Today, with its number of on-going various kind of social services and with a huge volunteering strength, Anand Ashram has become one of the leading NGOs of Vadodara.

About Anand Ashram and about all the beautiful angelic souls associated with it, there is so much to be written that it will take one separate book for its content.

Nature's Nature is to Give.

Nature has given us everything in abundance. It is up to us to utilize whatever is given to us. Moreover, whatever you do not utilize is taken back too. Anthropologists say that lakhs of years prior, human beings had a tail. Our tail-bone is the proof of it. Now, slowly slowly man stopped making any use of his tail and hence nature gradually eliminated it!

Kawal made an interesting observation in our garden. From the chilly plant, she used to pluck green chillies regularly. Once, enough stock of chillies was there in the kitchen and for few days she did not pluck them. She saw that new chillies had stopped growing and the old ones were dropping from the plant. New ones restarted growing once she again started plucking the old ones.

Similar is the case with money and all other resources. If you utilize and share your resources with those in need, it will grow. If you do not, it will not. I have complete faith in the saying that nobody has ever become poor by giving!

They say rich are getting richer. Why? Perhaps many of them know this secret that this is possible by giving. God loves the hands that give.

So, if you want to become rich or richer, be a giver! Of course, I don't say that you become a mindless giver. Give a portion of whatever you have, but give. Here, love and affection are important. The volume has no relevance at all.

God is always looking for angels who can carry out this work on his behalf. And mind well, this secret principle is not limited to money. It applies to all the pure feelings that are possessed by us – positivity, love, affection, compassion, knowledge.

Give knowledge if you are knowledgeable. If you do not have anything, you can at least give love which is more valuable than anything.

Once we know this secret and start giving, we are in sync with Nature's Nature!

Joy of Giving has no parallel!

Life becomes a celebration in its real sense when you experience this purest of the pure joy!

The secret revealed!

Nature's nature is that of a giver.

God is a giver.

Mother is a giver.

All that we need to do in life is to become a seeker first.

Seek from God first, then be a receiver. When you receive you can become a giver.

In fact, nature is waiting and looking for the seekers who in turn will become receivers and then givers.

To become a seeker, you need to have a clarity as to what you need from the universe. Whatever you demand, Universe will provide.

If you ask for the good, good will be given. If you ask for the bad, bad will be given.

He who understands this simple truth, will attune himself with God's power to give. Once you create a relation of love with Him, just imagine how much in abundance you can get!

So before asking, before demanding, before seeking, think how you are going to utilize it. In ancient times, *rishi-munis* used to do penance and ask for boons from God; these boons not necessarily were good ones all the times. At times they did ask for negative powers or bad boons which were given too!

So, this is the golden master key to success. Ask the right way and the whole universe will support you. What matters is your intensity.

Material things can be achieved also through this path. But utmost caution is necessary in it. We all know the story of King Midas and his Midas touch. He, without thinking, asked for the boon of golden touch. His food and water also started turning into gold!

Therefore, think as big as you can. Nature will give you. Dhirubhai Ambani is the modern-day example of how one can desire something with great intensity and achieve it. His tag lines *Kar lo duniya mutthi me, Only when you dream it, you can do it, Think big, think fast, think ahead* worked wonders and from a petrol pump attendant he became India's No.1 industrialist!

The tiny unit Hindustan Pharmaceuticals which become one of the role-model units of Gujarat was the result of dreaming big, aiming high combined with determined efforts to achieve it.

Yes, I had desired that I want to become popular.

As a student I had dreamt that when I graduate and start my own business, I should have an ultra-modern office with a beautiful secretary taking dictation from me.

Yes, I had desired that I should stay in a beautiful bungalow!

I did desire that I must possess imported cars!

He obliged! I was a seeker and he made me receiver.

Now it was my responsibility to become the giver. I started that and He started helping me by sending contributors at **Anand Ashram**. I became instrumental in serving the humanity.

Nimitta matra bhava Savyasachi is the essence of Shrimad Bhagwad Geeta!

When you become giver from receiver, you become His representative.

A human cannot imagine any higher achievement than this. And believe me, this is not difficult to achieve. Strong determination will do the magic. Try it!

When I was a student leader in college, I wanted to organise an inter-faculty debate and for its small budget of just Rs.1700 I was looking for a sponsor. I thought of approaching one of Vadodara's leading business tycoons, Shri Nanubhai Amin, owner of famous company Jyoti Limited. One day I gathered the courage and straightway went to his bungalow.

"Hey, what do you want?" Watchman stopped me at the gate.

"I want to meet Nanubhai sir." I told him.

"What's your name? Have an appointment?" he demanded.

"Tell him KS Chhabra has come to see you" without hesitation I replied.

I met Nanubhai and asked for a sponsor amount of Rs.1700. He readily agreed and asked me to get it from his office.

When I described my adventure to my college friends and committee, everyone laughed.

"Chhabra, you went to Nanubhai Amin, such a big shot, and asked only for Rs.1,700? You could have asked for 17,000!"

Similar is the case with the Big Boss up there! Increase your capacity to seek and if you ask it for 'giving', then He is bound to oblige.

I am writing this with my own experience with Anand Ashram. When I sold my business and decided to start an NGO, my family did have some apprehension that I may now spend all my savings towards sewa. But the magic of giving never let it happen. Whatever I had and whatever I desired for services of Anand Ashram from donors, went on increasing!

I can assure you from my own experience that if you decide to become a 'giver,' you become a net gainer. God sees to it that he who lives with the pure feeling of 'giving' never is a loser, never a sufferer.

Hence, I call it the 'master key'. If you want to become a gainer, be a giver. Once you become a giver, then it is God's responsibility not to let you down.

"Karmik" Account

Life has two forms: One is connected with limited breaths (Biological Body). Second relates to unending time (Amar Atma).

Here, by 'unending time' I mean your karma. Biological lives will go and come in various forms, but our Karmik Account is steadily maintained at one place! In our biological life we are connected with mundane, selfish things. In our sub-conscious the clock of our Karmik Account goes on ticking. It is like piggy bank of children. Whenever you do any sewa, your contribution is added into it. But here, the currency is love. The love given to others is matched in equivalent weightage by God in your Sewa Account.

This outlook will definitely enhance your life quality. The happiness of giving and if any re-birth is there, then it will be carried forward too.

I strongly feel that there should be a separate subject on Karma in school syllabus because values will be derived from this only. They will ultimately result in character building of individuals and good individuals means good society and a strong nation.

God gives us ample opportunities to write the pages of our book of life which we do by way of our deeds, or karma. But as Lord Krishna has said in Shrimad Bhagwad Geeta: *Karmanye vadhikaraste.........: You have a right to karma(actions) but never to any fruits thereof. You should never be motivated by the results of your karma, nor should there be any attachment in not doing your prescribed activities".*

This clearly means that God holds your future in His hands and those who are not ready for any unexpected turns in life crumble.

Always expect the unexpected. If you live with this clarity, you can take adversities in your stride.

Those who get this knowledge, their outlook towards life becomes conscious. A kind of awareness happens with knowledge.

LIFE DECODED

Every problem is an opportunity. When encountered with a problem, 'dis-cover' the problem and find the 'opportunity' lying in it. Ask during the dis-covering process: What is the problem? Why is the problem? Maybe it has arisen due to the manifestation of your own wish?

From outside, the problem may appear like a monster, but if you go closer, if you hug it, its form may change.

Decode the problem. It is certain that if you patiently try to understand and accept it maturely, that maturity will lead you to dis-cover the opportunity underlying in it.

When I had decided to commit suicide due to business setbacks and enormous debts, God had different designs for me and I met Guruji. A huge turning point came in life and my long pending wish of serving the humanity was fulfilled.

In our near fatal road accident, the whole family was saved. I remained immobile for three years due to multiple fractures in leg but I accepted my fate. Acceptance of His wish leads to mitigation of seemingly painful conditions. Along with God, I fell in love with my pain too, because that was given by Him! Here, the problem was pain. Opportunity was to uplift myself.

God makes us struggle to dis-cover the hidden diamond under the coal. Those who complain and throw it away will never gain happiness like those who accept the situation and convert the difficulties into blessing.

If you are a student, look at this interesting fact this way: are you weak in Maths? Science? Explore and sharpen your other strengths. Everyone is gifted with something or the other. Hence, all comparisons are also false. Fish should not be judged by its non-ability to climb a tree. Fish is not programmed to climb tree. Similarly, a monkey is not programmed to live under water.

Have no regrets in life. If you live with honesty and truthfulness, there will not be a single occasion in your life to have any regret. This is because you will be in sync with the law of nature. I had regrets for long of using tricks to pass the exams and not having met my dying cousin sister. But eventually I got rid of them when the realization happened that whatever happens, happens for a purpose.

Honesty and truthfulness are the golden keys which will open up the treasures of life and bring us laurels.

Have faith. Don't worry about the future. He knows the best about it. Just don't hinder your own path which has been charted for you by God.

River of life is flowing fast towards His ocean

I now feel that with so many committed and talented people connected with Anand Ashram, perhaps a momentum has got created by the force of which the institution can continue even without me.

In my prayers to my Bhagwanji I have been expressing to him:

"I am done with all my responsibilities. Any more is an additional bonus. Now the river of my life is eager to submerge with your vast ocean."

Bhagwanji keeps on repeating: "I know better! There are still some projects which you will have to complete. **Big Sewa Dream is one of them.**"

Incidentally, Big Sewa Dream is a dream visualised by Anand Ashram to create an actual 'sewa-campus'. Land for this proposed campus is already in Anand Ashram's possession. We have named it as "Swarg" – the heaven which is going to be Happiness Home for the Senior Citizens. Kind hearted donors are invited and requested to support its creation.

The sewa campus Swarg will have 'Ashirwad Bhavan', accommodation facility for the elderly, 'Anand Bhavan', 'Happiness Centre', 'Kutirs' and much more. It will have all the ultra-modern facilities with centralised Wellness Centre and Kitchen. All efforts will be made to create a self-sustained ecosystem, addressing the need of environmental sensitivity.

Special mention of a multi-talented person, Pradeep Bhinde, who has authored this book for me, is needed. When I came to know about his creativity, I had expressed to him that Ishwarji has sent yet another angel to me as an asset to Anand Ashram. He has proved me right.

I strongly feel that with everyone we meet in life, there must be some connections, somewhere in past births, of which we are not aware. Mysteries of life are enchanting!

Coincidences also perhaps have some connections somewhere. I could co-relate my accident that resulted in my broken femur to the thought of an American Cultural Anthropologist Margaret Mead when recently, I read a post on Facebook by a dear friend Gaurang Joshipura, an excerpt of her interview taken many years back. She was asked by a student what was the first sign of civilization in a culture.

Mead said that that the first sign of civilization in ancient culture was a femur (thighbone) that had been broken and then healed. Mead explained that in animal kingdom, if you break your leg, you die. You cannot run from danger, get to the river for a drink or hunt for food. You are meat for prowling beasts. No animal survives a broken leg long enough for the bone to heal.

A broken femur that has healed is the evidence that someone has taken time to stay with the one who fell, has bound up the wound, has carried the person to safety and has tended the person to recovery.

"Helping someone else through difficulty is where civilization starts" Meads said. **We are at our best when we help others.** Be civilized!

The intention of writing my life story is to inspire more and more people, especially the youth of today to come forward and extend their helping hand to the needy in whatever way they can. It is also intended to inspire people to practise and master the knack of turning each adversity into opportunity.

Towards the end of my life story, with overflowing love in my heart and with folded hands always praying for the suffering humanity, I reproduce below a quote, a translation of an old Sanskrit shloka, from a book by Sudha Murty that perfectly echoes my feelings as my no more demands are pending with Him now:

"O God, I don't need a kingdom, nor do I desire to be an emperor. I don't want rebirth or the golden vessels or heaven. I don't need anything from you. O Lord, if you want to give me something, then give me soft heart and hard hands, so that I can wipe the tears of others."

When I look back at my sewa-journey so far, I do feel satisfied with the tremendous progress Anand Ashram has made in various kinds of social services. Of course, this would not have been possible without

His grace, family support, especially the rock-like support of Kawal, my wife and all my dear friends and the dedicated volunteers whose unconditional love is my real strength.

But *picture abhi baki hai* friends! Before I depart and meet my creator above, I want to leave a trail of love, affection, emotion, and dedication for the happiness of fellow-travellers in this journey and also for the souls who will come after my departure. This wish will be fulfilled when my big dream, the Big Sewa Dream "Swarg" – the actual sewa-campus as described in previous pages above, takes its real form.

शुभं भवतु!

12.

The Big Sewa Dream

Corporates have business dreams, I have big sewa dreams.

Our thoughts can take actual form only if they are first conceptualised in mind and then acted upon.

Dreams turn into reality only if we dream first and chase them.

God, Almighty, Existence...created us and sent to this beautiful planet to experience, to celebrate, to learn and to transcend this beautiful journey called "Life!"

At one stage or other, everyone intuitively gets the insight that he or she is here not only to live and leave, but the creator has put something on stake on each and every individual.

Since last few years, I have been constantly feeling that NOW is the time for me to take the big leap. Rather, a huge leap in the direction of serving the suffering humanity.

I get visualisations of suffering souls looking with hope in their eyes.

The biggest, the ultimate dream is yet to be fulfilled, and that is The Big Sewa Dream: the creation of Anand Ashram Sewa Campus.

Underlying thought behind visualising this dream is to create an exclusive sewa-campus which will be practically useful to lonely elders, differently abled people and other such suffering beings. Industrial, Educational, and other such campuses are many, but the concept of establishing a sewa-campus is unique.

Hence, Anand Ashram is on its way to establish a self-contained, self-sustained actual *sewa* campus Happiness Home "Swarg," as we have named it. Swarg, the Big Sewa Dream, the heaven on earth, will have under its umbrella everything that all beings wish to accomplish: "To Live Life Beyond Life."

Swarg is coming up near Bamangam village in Anand District of Gujarat.

Here is an overview of its planning.

Ashirwad Bhawan

Suitable staying arrangement for the elderly who suffer either financially, medically, emotionally or all together.

Anand Bhawan

This will be The Happiness Centre with an Auditorium, Meditation and Prayer Hall, Meeting Hall and other such facilities where one can uplift the spirits to the highest levels.

Kutirs

Beautiful cottages for those who wish to spend their life in peace, joy and sewa-celebration.

Swarg will have its own Physiotherapy Centre, Recreation Hall, Library, Education Centre, Skill Centre with latest digital aids, Sports Facilities, Wellness Centre, Parking, Community Kitchen and much more.

Use of solar energy, organic farming, rain water harvesting, lush green gardens and greenery all around the campus will be integral part of Swarg.

Living with an ecosystem.

Self-sustenance. Assistance. Accessibility for all. Boosting self-esteem.

And last but not the least, Love and Compassion are the driving force by which this dream can be fulfilled.

Of course, huge investment and efforts are required before this dream can turn into reality.

Anand Ashram Charitable Trust and all key and high potential donors and supporters shall be custodians of this project and virtual trustees of this sewa.

I am certain, as *Bhagwanji* has inspired us to take a plunge once again in this herculean sewa-task, He is bound to send the required help too! Such help is solicited from the Corporates – from their CSR budgets, from the Government – from the people's welfare funds, individual philanthropists, donors and from welfare-focussed like-minded people. The sewa campus will be of the people, by the people and for the people.

The dream will be fulfilled with the help of Almighty and all well-wishers of humanity.

My trust in Him and His manifestation, the humanity, is total.

With deep love in my heart, I pray to God to bless us with more strength to contribute to the suffering humanity.

Shri KS Chhabra in one of his meetings with Shri Narendra Modiji

Shri Narendra Modiji's appreciation of Shri KS Chhabra for his contribution to the society

cm/apro/13012006

Snehi Shree Chhabraji,

Saprem Namaskar.

I am thankful to you and Rotary Club of Baroda Jawaharnagar for undertaking revamping of the crematorium – MOKSHDHAM.

Our 'Sanskruti' has been society – oriented. Where as, in other parts of the world, people depend on government and official measures for the welfare of the society, we have since time immortal, cultivated a tradition, wherein, people's participation makes these measures possible.

Rotary Clubs, allover the world, have been in forefront in rendering selfless and devoted services to the society. I appreciate the projects under taken by Rotary Club of Baroda Jawaharnagar for the welfare of the humanity.

I assure you my heartiest support in your endeavor to make VADODARA a wonder-city.

Thank you .

(Narendra Modi)

To,
Shree K. S. Chhabra - President,
Rotary Club of Baroda, Jawaharnagar,
911-912, Siddharth Comlex, R.C Dutt Road, Alkapuri,
Vadodara – 390 007.

Narendra Modi
Chief Minister, Gujarat State

Pradeep Bhinde

Pradeep Bhinde is a poet, content writer, translator, radio artist, singer.

An excellent compere, he works as Honorary CEO with Anand Ashram Charitable Trust to provide creative help with his multi-skilled abilities. He is engaged in number of social services of the Trust too.

Pradeep is blessed with initiation into *sannyas* by Osho himself!

Just as pearls become necklace after polishing, arranging and binding, just as beautiful flowers become garland with an articulate touch, he created this book with his absorbing writing style after jotting down series of narrations by Shri KS Chhabra.

The fragrance of his bouquet of beautiful words is going to leave the reader filled with joy in addition to feeling inspired.

For him, in his own words, the process of this beautiful creation was nothing less than deep meditation, a flight to ever bliss.

This book is the outcome of bridge of love between KS and Pradeep.

*

pradeep.bhinde@gmail.com

M: 9974012031

And on that Dawn, a Star was born!

And on that dawn, a Star was born,
In a golden sac, so many look upon!
Your care, your warmth, your knowledge, we adore,
The strength, the determination, the inspiration you abode.
You show us the silver lining in the deepest cloud,
As a friend and guide your love has no bound.
Smile when the times are hard we have learnt,
As joy and sorrow come in equals in the knowledge we have earned.
A leader like you with so much passion,
A rigour to serve the Humanity and the Nation.
We are so proud of you and thankful to the Lord,
To have a Dad with the mightiest Heart.
And on that dawn, a Star was born,
In a golden sac, so many look upon!

We Love you Lots & Lots Papa,

Namrata and Amrit

Book Reviews

Congratulations KS Ji! Book is an amazing reading material and gives insight of a common man's journey from student to businessman and finally to philanthropist!

– Shaju CO, CEO-Best Value Chem

* * *

At the outset, it is very difficult to write as a ghost-writer on someone else's life. It requires patience and the ability to extricate insights.

Shri Pradeep Bhinde has managed admirably to weed out the internal secrets (or memories, painful as they may be) and transformed them into chapters of wisdom and spiritual learnings. Each chapter has nuggets of self-help for all of us to imbibe into our daily spiritual lives.

To me, this is the epicentre of the success of the book, credit to the man's forthrightness notwithstanding.

The book is an honest, open hearted look into Mr Chhabra's life right from his birth to his standing in society today covering 6 + decades of ups and downs in the journey of his discovery towards enlightenment.

The read through chapters was a like a gently flowing river, twisting and turning with all eddies and currents but bringing joy, solace and peace in the end.

– Ashish Pandya, Vice President, Reliance Retail

* * *

Thanks for a marvellous gift "In Love with Humanity." I read the book very minutely with definite purpose. This is inspiring biography of a *devdoot* of God. The language. narrations and presentation of poet singer Pradeepbhai are lucid – flowing like river full with fragrance of a great soul. Present generation younger or elder will derive principles Love, Affection, Dedication, Concern, Faith, Determination etc and they will be motivated to implement these values in their life.

–Prof. Pravinchandra Thakkar, Ex Director &
Vice Chancellor, Lokbharati

* * *

"ज़िंदगी बड़ी होनी चाहिए लंबी नहीं" ऐसा "आनंद" फिल्म में राजेश खन्ना ने कहा। लेकिन मैं छाबरा जी को केवल लंबी ज़िंदगी की दुआ देता हूं। क्योंकि उनकी जिंदगी बड़ी तो है ही, विस्तृत भी है। कितने लोगों तक उनका प्यार भरा स्पर्श पहुंचा है। उनकी खिलखिलाहट के भंवर में कितने ही लोग आ चुके हैं।

The aura of his personality is so bright that you get attracted and attached to it instantly.

The book "In Love with Humanity" is a revelation and we all will connect with this book after going through a few pages. The book so beautifully brought up by Pradeep Bhindeji is worth reading, not once but again and again. I personally connect with his journey half way in the book and am trying to follow the rest of the path, God willing. And I do hope his conviction, that what you wish from your heart will surely happen, comes true for me, too.

A must read.

– Sanjeev Ratti, Leading Businessman and Social Activist, Trustee-Anand Ashram Charitable Trust

* * *

I read through the book thoroughly enjoying each part described. As I moved ahead of each page, I could see the different kaleidoscopic visions of a man who started his life as a humble normal human to become a man of integrity.

One could probe into the intricacies of a man's psyche who struggled emotionally, physically and each time giving his God, the credit, and a driving force to overcome his weak moments.

Certain parts touched my heart emotionally and brought tears to my eyes. The part where you have wholeheartedly given credit to Mrs. Chhabra for being a strong pillar and an embodiment of support made me feel proud. Coming from a man was worth the praise.

Your adventurous nature, your playing truant, your open acceptance of weak points love angle made me smile and think, our man is a normal human despite all his dynamism.

Your success is your doing. Your flamboyancy is contagious and your dream realised, is your gift from God and blessings from such lovely spiritually oriented parents. Kudos to a successful man.

Pradeepji congratulations for beautifully shaping and carving Chhabraji's colourful story in such a panoramic view with quotes, each part described *par excellence.* Congratulations Mr. Multitalented! A big Salute to you too!

– Kumkum Bhardwaj,
Academician, Writer, Poetess

* * *

"Learn from the experiences, then forget the past and always look ahead to create a happy life" "Target the moon so that even if you miss, you fall among the start". "*Jo prapt hai, wo paryapt hai*" Such and other motivational quotes and events in life of Shri KS Chhabra teach us a new definition of life. Language, arrangement of chapters and the flow of the book are *par excellence.* This unputdownable book is capable of inspiring people of all ages. A wonderful book without any doubt.

– Ripalkumar Parikh, Journalist & Columnist, Gujarat Vandan Weekly

* * *

Thanks for the wonderful book. Already falling in love with humanity all the more after reading few pages. Quite lucidly written and amazing quotes!! Truly a treasure of motivation.

– CA Harsh Rathi, Leading Chartered Accountant

* * *

Like flowers when they bloom, they spread fragrance. You are now that fragrance and your work for humanity has become sacred.

I am sure God is vouching you and giving light to each act of yours. I don't have any words to express how I feel today looking at your humanitarian work. Salute.

– Preeti Chandan, Spiritual Leader

* * *

The book "In Love with Humanity" is narration by Shri Pradeep Bhinde...which was as tasty to my mind as vegetable cream soup to my tongue.

It reveals the process of sliding into path of perpetual happiness ...by becoming a seeker...to a receiver...and finally to a giver i.e. the representative of God.

The idea of "Karma Theory" into the syllabus of school education is innovative and explosive." Man is selfish by nature" – says Hobbs... but... What the society will become if most of the people will understand that the self-interest is served best when they flow with Nature's nature...which is "giving".

I wish that Chhabra ji's this dream comes true soon and gen next falls into "In Love with humanity" in their own self-interest.

The life story of Chhabra ji is inspiring... the book motivates for a change in attitude...it pushes the reader towards sewa activities. which means sailing towards "Anand"..the ultimate desire of every one of us.

I strongly recommend everyone to read this book very earnestly and light a lamp of wisdom in their life.

– Sarvesh Rastogi, Academician,
Career Counsellor.

* * *

A lovely Life dedicated to humanity!!

Indeed, I am referring to the biography of Shri K.S. Chhabraji which has been so meticulously & aptly interwoven in words by our Pradeep Bhindeji.

I know K.S. ji since more than two decades, yet, some interesting unknown life incidents were a treat to read.

The incidents & anecdotes are so interesting that I completed the book at one late night sitting and that too after a hectic day of work. Being human and inspiring thousands of people to the humanitarian deeds is an amazing achievement by K.S.ji. Only a pure soul with noble intentions can achieve such a wonderful feat. I also admire K.S.ji's exemplary & passionate oratory skill that spell bounds the listener. My best wishes for many many more incredible achievements in the bright and blessed future!!

– Jayesh Pande, Executive Engineer, Water Development Agency, Govt of India.

* * *

Amazing motivational book "In Love with Humanity" showing different colors of Chhabra Sir. Mr. Bhinde has also done a greatt job. Congratulations.

– Preeti Shrivastav, Academician, Founder-Chairperson of Jeevan Mulya

* * *

Each page has fragrance of Shri Chhabra Sir's motivational life journey. I found chapter 'Stable and Able' The Best in which writer Pradeepji has beautifully described beginning of Sir's spiritual journey arising out of darkest night to a bright sunrise with Guruji Shri G. Narayana's blessings. A 'must-read' gripping book.

– Dr. Vandana Srivastava, Social Activist, Children Meditation facilitator

* * *

Beautiful book with inspirational events written in the style of an interesting novel. Hats off to Shri KS Chhabra Sir and yes, of course the writer Shri Pradeep Bhinde for a classic creation!

– Sandhya Pandey, Principal

* * *

What a motivational and inspiring biography. Shri Chhabra sir has been our role-model in sewa activities. Reading this book, we came to know about how such great people struggle in life and then come out as winner and leaders. Hats off!

– Santvana Chaturvedi, Academician.

* * *

Good presentation, simple but very appealing language. Nice and apt quotes by Osho, Mother Teressa, and others. Use of good songs. Overall worth of all praise. Congrats for your amicable efforts.

– Dr Shivkumar Shukla, Scientist, Sarabhai Chemicals

* * *

Really inspiring and straight from the horse's mouth experiences of life, a path of simplicity and devotion, a path undertaken for selfless service

– Hoston Thomas, Leading Industrialist

* * *

Today I completed reading your biography. Firstly, thanks to Pradeep uncle who took an initiative to write a book on your life experiences. I am glad that I got a chance to learn about you in detail. Since, childhood I always saw you as happy – go – lucky kind of person. I never knew about challenges behind your smiling face. Reading about your struggle has motivated me to take life easily and have faith in God. Your journey reflects how truly you were supported and protected by almighty. This has made me think that Babaji is also with me in every situation. Moreover, your desire and contribution towards humanity has questioned my existence. Really, you are gem of a person. Your feelings towards sewa are appreciated.

– Ms. Manmeet Bagga, Academician

* * *

My observation is that "It is very difficult to be so dedicated to a cause of being good to others and that too in this world full of hatred, spite & selfish motives". that's why I admire this man who has transcended multiple levels – from an entrepreneur – industrialist to a messenger of goodwill.

– Chandresh Makhija, Leading Businessman

* * *

"Extremely Impressive. It depicts the interesting journey of how you (Chhabraji) progressed in life from childhood to what you are today. Magnanimous. Awesome. Wow! Tusi Great Ho Sir Ji. Wishing I could be 1% of what you are! Ultimate Seva to Humanity to the core and seva with purity of thoughts, love and intentions to serve the society. You should be nominated for Nobel Prize by Govt of India for the great selfless service to the society."

– Rakesh Narula, Leading Businessman

* * *

www.ingramcontent.com/pod-product-compliance
Lightning Source LLC
LaVergne TN
LVHW091324150826
845673LV00006B/1767

* 9 7 9 8 8 9 1 3 3 6 1 1 7 *